D1051084

Stories *of* Love

&

Psychotherapy

Kenneth Jedding

To Martha,

My first teacher
and good friend,

XO
2021 Ken

Copyright © 2021 by Kenneth Jedding

ISBN #978-1-7363445-8-3

Cover drawing by Terry Rosenberg
Photography by John Bigelow Taylor

Copyedit by Emma Moylan
Typeset/cover design by Michael Grossman

Font: Filosofia

This is a work of fiction. Unless otherwise indicated, all the names, characters, businesses, places, events and incidents in this book are either the product of the author's imagination or used in a fictitious manner. Any resemblance to actual persons, living or dead, or actual events is purely coincidental.

For Bette and Joan

CONTENTS

Love   7

    Claims   9

    The Sadism of
    Red and White   33

    Sirens   49

Illusion   75

    Ghosts   83

    The Ropes   101

Recovery   147

    The Forgiving   149

    Reconstructions   177

Afterword   217

Acknowledgments   221

LOVE

Claims

The Sadism of Red and White

Sirens

These seven fictional stories are about how people psychologically live their lives, how they yearn, sacrifice and love.

Carl Jung said, "Life addresses questions to us, and we ourselves are a question."

The first three stories are about the unusual forms that love takes, both in the world of a therapist's office, and beyond.

CLAIMS

(Jack, Kara)

I

Jack arrived for his first session with his psychotherapist, Robert, and he stopped in the doorway. He was in his seventies and his face was drawn. Then he slowly came in and sat down.

"I'm a lawyer," Jack said. "Do you believe in God?"

"Sort of," Robert said.

"What do you think happens after one dies?"

"I believe the soul survives."

"What does that even mean?" Jack said.

"I don't know. What do you think happens after one dies?"

"Fade to black," Jack said. "I don't believe in anything, but I'm looking for a therapist who does. I went to three people before you."

"You asked what happens after one dies and they asked you the same question without answering?" Robert said.

"Exactly."

"But I just asked you a question, too."

"You answered first," Jack said. "You're in."

Jack was facing Robert, sitting in one of the two saddle-leather chairs. In the office, there was an Italian-designed navy-blue sofa between them to the side, a navy-woven carpet, and two windows that looked out on an antique store on 11th Street in Greenwich Village.

They sat in silence for two minutes, a long time.

Jack's eyes finally met Robert's. He said quietly, "I have fourth-stage pancreatic cancer. I'm dying."

"I'm so sorry."

"Do you know, I'm one of the most powerful lawyers in New York?" he said, and he stood and walked to the door.

"We still have forty minutes," Robert said.

"See you same time, next week," Jack said as if making an executive decision, and he left.

□ □ □

"Sorry about last time," Jack said as he settled in, the following Wednesday. "My wife lectured me ... She gave me this red journal; wants me to write down my thoughts." Then he smiled, giving Robert a sense of who he used to be. "Let's try again."

"Let's," Robert said.

"I've been home from work for three months. I've had time to think, some issues I'd like to discuss. I guess you could say I want a second opinion. All right?"

Robert nodded.

"Let's begin with my ex-wife, Eleanor. Twenty years ago, she cheated on me and I left her. But when I look back on it, I know why she did it."

"Why?"

"Guess."

"I have no idea, Jack," Robert said.

"Do you know? I've been home, watching *I Love Lucy* reruns," he said. "She was really very funny, by the way. I completely forgot ... Anyway, I'll just launch in. That's what people do here, in therapy, right?"

"Yes."

"So, this is what I remembered," Jack said. "When I was a kid, I always used to ask my mother if she liked me. Can you imagine? She wasn't happy with my father; maybe she cheated on him, I don't know, but I used to say, 'Do you like me?' The bottom line: I never felt that she loved me. Strange thing to realize—now ... I transferred that feeling to my ex, Eleanor, so I threw myself into my work. We have two kids and I was never there ... The point is this: Eleanor was right to cheat. She married the guy. That's her husband now. I believe I owe her an apology, after all this time. What do you think?"

"Could be," Robert said.

"I'm a good amateur therapist, wouldn't you say? ... I think it's important to get it right; to know yourself, even if you're twenty years late," he said. Robert nodded.

Jack smiled softly. "Do you know? I have a new wife now, Kara. She's younger," he continued. "I married again after all that drama. She's why I'm really here, Robert. It's Robert, right?"

"Yes."

"She's the one I really want to talk to you about."

"Oh?"

"She's angry at me," Jack said.

"Why?"

"There's this lawyer, Sean, a colleague in the office. I told her I wouldn't mind if she slept with him."

□ □ □

Jack told Robert his story.

He'd met Kara when she joined the firm. She'd graduated from Columbia Law, served as a law clerk for a federal judge, and spent over a decade as a prosecutor in the U.S. Attorney's Office of the Southern District of New York. She came in as a full partner.

Kara and Jack were both divorced, she thirty-nine—she was briefly married in her early twenties—and Jack fifty-nine. "The age difference made the idea of us as a couple too unlikely for either to take seriously," he said.

They dined together at business dinners and golfed together at charity tournaments. As they grew fond of each other, they camouflaged their friendship with father-daughter style camaraderie. "I invited her to go shopping and help me choose gifts for my girlfriends," Jack said. "She'd take my arm and tell me to buy the beige Cuccinelli sweater, the Hermes gold bracelet, or the turquoise Loro Piana scarf. One day, I shopped alone and returned to work with a freshwater pearl necklace. 'Try it on,' I said, and Kara did. I know she imagined for the briefest of moments that the gift was for her. It wasn't.

"On long walks, Kara would ask me what I thought of her boyfriends. Occasionally, I'd put my arm around her. All of her troubles with men amused me so. Did I find any of her boyfriends suitable? As it turns out, no, I didn't. Steve drank too much, this guy, Arthur, he had too much debt, and there was Brian, who was too close to his ex. But then Mike came along, and I couldn't find anything wrong with him." He smiled at Robert. "Not for lack of trying!

"We had lunch together. And one night, dinner; sushi. I remember she wore jeans and a T-shirt. Then, over the holidays I suggested dinner at La Grenouille, and this time she wore pearls, a black dress and heels.

"At the end of the night, outside of her apartment and in view of her doorman, I kissed her goodnight. On the cheek. I was a gentleman, Robert. No pawing, just respect," Jack said. "Another dinner followed, at Orso after seeing a Pinter play on Broadway, and at the end of the night I kissed her for real.

"You know, a dare began to play out in both of our minds: How odd it would be for us to fall in love? This became, let's do it just to show ourselves how silly it is. We knew it was reversible, after all, even cliché. We assumed we'd eventually come to our senses and find age-appropriate partners. Yet we were having so much fun in the meantime.

"The first time we had sex, we found it amusing. Kara said she told her sister, 'We actually laughed, Anne. We're just having fun.' But the next time we didn't laugh. And the third time, well, we were hungry for each other's mouths and bodies.

"When Kara joined the firm, I learned that she thought I was one of the best legal minds in New York. I am, you know, Robert. She told me it was a jump for her to see me as more. But things continued to develop.

"One day I brought a bouquet of peonies and put them on a common table outside of her office to be discreet. She walked out and I said, 'Just to freshen things up around here,' as if I believed it. And I think I was blushing. From that moment on, she was all in. She'd later confess: the peonies and the blushing sealed the deal.

"We married at City Hall. We reasoned that a City Hall wedding wasn't quite real. We were still on the lam.

"Kara and I have been married for sixteen years."

□ □ □

"I won't be in therapy for much longer," Jack said at the start of the next session. "We're going to be doing a new round of chemo. So I need to discuss a few things."

"All right."

"First, I wonder how Kara will remember me when I'm gone. When I consider the question, I become furious."

"Why?"

"Because I won't be here. Because her life goes on. It's one of the insults inherent in marrying a woman twenty years younger. I mentioned to you I told her she could sleep with Sean, this guy at work."

"Why did you tell her that again, Jack?"

"Because she's going to do it one day anyway," he said. "This way, maybe I won't feel so totally shut out. I know him, he's a great guy, just transferred here from LA."

"So you're angry that she's going to survive you, but you're telling her to leave on some level?"

"I don't see it that way. Not at all."

"How do you see it?" Robert said.

"I'm dealing with my illness," and then he said, "I can't feel that she cares about me. Not really."

"But what did she say when—"

"—Tell me about God," Jack interrupted.

Robert thought for a moment and said, "It's kind of a mystery, Jack. To me, the interesting thing is to keep getting closer to whatever it is, like a moth circling a flame."

"You say it's a mystery? I don't have time for mysteries," Jack said. "What happens after people die?"

"I don't know, Jack."

"I find the prospect appalling. It's not just about leaving, though if I think too much of my kids, I'll go crazy. It's about what remains. What kind of mark I'll leave ...

"I'm going to go see Eleanor," Jack continued. "I need to get things straight with her," and he spent the rest of the session talking about his first marriage: how she'd cheated, how he'd left her, and how she'd raised the kids.

Jack called her and they met at Sant Ambroeus on the Upper East side.

"You don't look too good, Jack," Eleanor said, as she sat down.

"I'm not," Jack said. They ordered cappuccinos and scones.

"The kids are keeping me up to date," she said.

"How are they taking this?"

"I don't think it's hit them yet."

"They stay away," Jack said. "They'll get zapped, eventually. You'll look after them, right?"

"Of course."

"You always did," he said.

"How's your young girl? Eleanor said. "This must be rough on her." Jack nodded. She began to speak and Jack blurted out, "I'm sorry, Ellie."

"For what, Jack?"

"I wasn't there for you."

"I cheated on you, Jack," Eleanor said.

"It doesn't matter. Do you accept my apology?"

She slowly nodded her head.

"We're in a different world now," Jack said after he described the meeting to Robert in the next session. "But do you know what's strange? She forgave me, and now it feels like she won't remember me at all."

"I don't understand," Robert said.

"Maybe a grudge would have been more of a claim. Isn't that a better way for people to remember you after you're gone? If they're at peace with you, well, they'll forget."

"Love, affection, those can make a claim too, no?" Robert said.

"Not as much as a grudge can." He looked at Robert for a moment and said, "I'm tired ... It's so humiliating."

Jack stood and walked to the door, and he stopped and shrugged. And spontaneously, Robert moved to him and they hugged goodbye.

That was the last time Robert would ever see him.

Jack was a no-show the next week, and Robert called and left a message. The following Wednesday he called again, this time on Jack's home number, and a woman picked up.

"I'm a friend of Jack's," Robert said, preserving Jack's confidentiality, and he gave his name.

"No, you're not a friend, you're his therapist," she said. "I'm his wife, Kara. Jack's gone."

"He died?"

"Yes."

"I'm so sorry," Robert said, and they didn't speak.

After a moment of silence, Kara said, "Thank you, Robert," and she hung up.

II

Relationships in therapy are intense but, after a time, people leave. That is an adjustment for therapists, as it was for Robert, especially early on. Some of his patients regarded him as a functional technician, as they might, say, an electrician or a plumber. They'd get the help they needed and disappear, or they might send a voicemail or a text: "Thank you, but I won't be needing you anymore." The treatment would end and Robert would have to psychologically shift, as he would in reaction to any severed relationship.

But here, the calculus changed. Jack would never be back. Jack had trusted him, a stranger, in the last month of his life. He wondered what claim Jack might have on him, and whom Jack would be to him now.

Before he left the office, he googled Jack's *Times* obituary. It listed some of his high-stakes cases. Robert smiled, feeling that Jack would have been pleased with the notice.

Then he put the paper away.

Jack was gone.

Robert stopped on the way home in a gourmet market to buy some lamb for dinner. As he was being served, he heard a man yell piercingly, "Hey!"

He turned. The man—Robert guessed, he was an old eighty-five—was trying to get service at the nearby fish counter, and was yelling at the Black teen who was attempting to wait on him.

"You didn't go to school, did you? You're not very smart, are you?" the man crowed. The kid was startled, and Robert sensed that it was his first job.

Robert approached and, as if watching himself from outside of his own body, he put an admonishing finger in front of the old man's face, and said, "Don't you ever talk to him that way. Or to anyone. Ever. Again."

The old man turned to Robert. "Oh yeah, motherfucker?" he said. "Why don't you mind your own business?" and then, "I can take you!" and he raised his fists and became red in the face, screaming, "Put 'em up!"

Robert felt like he was in a B movie.

"What are you waiting for?" the man said, moving into Robert's space, less than a foot away. Robert towered over him and thought, I can grab him by the lapels of his jacket. He visualized how that would intimidate the old man, or calm him down, and he was about to do it, but then a kind of auto-pilot kicked in, and he simply turned and walked away. He took his place on the checkout line in another part of the store.

It was an ordinary Wednesday, a beautiful summer evening, about, what? seventy-eight degrees and it was 7:12 p.m. All lovely and forgettable, Robert thought. Yet waiting to pay for his groceries, he could still feel the man's anger. He knew that the evening was begging to morph into a different time scheme; that of having this stranger on his mind every day for years to come. As a lover might say, "You'll think of me always," for things could have gone differently: the old man could have had a heart attack just from the way he was screaming, or certainly if he, Robert, had grabbed him by the lapels. And although everyone in the store knew the old man was out of line, Robert wondered what they would have thought if the man had died and clock time changed into psychological time.

Robert asked himself, what would I have thought a day later, or two weeks, or two years later? You let an old man draw you into a confrontation? But he'd walked away. The man had no claim on him. People don't retain their hold on you, he thought.

He paid for his groceries and went outside.

On the street, he felt the sun on his face. He passed a gelato store but he wouldn't have any. He and his wife would be eating dinner soon. But he enjoyed seeing those in the store, mostly Chinese exchange students from NYU Shanghai who seemed to congregate there.

III

A year passed.

One day, Robert had a session with a new patient. She entered Robert's office, a blond woman in a white blouse, a navy skirt and heels. She sat down and said, "You don't know me, but I didn't want to tell you who I was on the phone. I made the appointment using my maiden name."

Robert waited.

"I'm Jack Harris's widow, Kara."

Robert knew he had to say something but he sat there, dumbfounded. Kara seemed to sense his predicament and said, "We spoke briefly on the phone that time."

Robert nodded.

"I saw another therapist after Jack died. I cried for months and months, grieved as I was supposed to, and then I felt that I could move on. And I've been OK since then— at least, as much as I can be, but something came up," she said and her eyes became moist. "Do you think you can treat me?"

"I don't know, Kara. If I treated you, I'd respect Jack's confidentiality."

"Things you couldn't say?"

"Yes."

"I'm a lawyer," Kara said. "I have confidentiality with my clients as well. But Jack mentioned you and I wanted to see someone who knew him."

"Let's talk for a bit and see how we both feel," Robert said.

"All right ... Do you know: I went to NYU a thousand years ago. I haven't been back to Washington Square Park in, well, decades. This area was very special to me. I walked through the park before meeting you today."

"What did you study?"

"Liberal arts, but then I shifted to courses that I thought would help me get into law school."

Robert was silent.

"Here's the thing," Kara continued. "When I met Jack, we were ridiculously mismatched. He was twenty years older. I always thought I wanted a man to take care of me, not financially, necessarily, but to be there. But twenty years? As we became involved and we married, I thought, I'm going to outlive him, but then I forgot it. We both did. But when he got sick, that same thought, that I'd outlive him, made me angry. And he was angry, too.

"Jack told me to date other men," Kara continued. "Specifically, he told me to date my colleague, Sean. Not date. Sleep with. Can you believe it? He said, 'I was a '60s guy, it's all right,'" and she rolled her eyes. "So crazy! I want to solve this. Why did he say that?"

Robert shrugged.

"So do you know what I did? I slept with one of my old boyfriends, Dan, while Jack was still alive. Can you imagine that? Daddy's little harlot." She took a deep breath. "I was OK with it at the time. In life we get angry and we do things, right? And Jack sort of asked me to do it. My previous therapist told me it was a way for me to deal with our mortality, mine or Jack's; to distance myself."

Robert leaned back in his chair and he thought, No, I definitely won't treat her.

"But then I found this," Kara said, and she pulled out a small red book. "I gave this to him as a gift, for Jack to keep a journal, though he only wrote on one page. I don't know if he intended for me to find it. Maybe he did."

She sat up straighter.

"I'd like to read you something, I hope you don't mind."

I do mind, Robert thought; Jack told me everything he wanted to tell me. I don't need to hear more about Jack from you.

She opened the book. "It's right here," she said, and she read, "'I never felt loved, not by my mother, not by Ellie,' his first wife, 'nor even by Kara.'"

She carefully closed the red journal and put it back in her handbag. Then she said, "Did he intend for me to find this?"

Robert looked at her for a moment. Then he said, "I'll treat you, Kara. And we'll try to figure these things out."

□ □ □

A week passed and when Kara entered for the next session, her gait was lighter. "Hi!" she said, and she fell into the chair, exuberant.

"What's going on?" Robert said, smiling.

"I don't want to talk about heavy things today. Do you?"

Robert laughed. "Heavy things are what I do," he said.

"Remember how bad I felt last time?"

"Yes," Robert said.

"Well, I went to Washington Square Park before the session and I was able to leave it all behind," Kara said. "Do you understand? When I walk through the park, it redeems me."

"What do you mean?" Robert said.

"I told you. I was an undergraduate at NYU. It all came back to me."

"How so?"

She met Robert's eyes for a moment and smiled warmly. "One day when I was a freshman," she began, "I remember: I was sitting on the lip of the fountain. I was waiting for a guy I'd seen in class, Michael. I'd kissed him on the cheek and we'd made a plan to meet. Then I'd run back to my dorm and said to my roommate, 'I need more cleavage!'" Kara laughed and so did Robert. "She lent me her tank top.

"I sat at the fountain and I knew Michael might show up or he might not, but do you know what? It didn't matter," she said. "By our meeting in class and my little kiss on his cheek, I knew I'd locked it in; he'd be in touch one way or the other. I knew we'd get to know each other, hang out, eat Chinese food, have sex"—and again, she laughed—"and, yes, I'd even get to wear his green tartan shirt. He was going to be mine, Robert, and it was guileless, because we liked each other, and it was right."

She took a deep breath and looked to be far away. "So I sat there that day. I felt the breeze in my hair, heard the fountain, looked at the trees, the flowers, the squirrels, and maybe I even opened up my textbook and studied for a half hour, I don't remember. But I knew the wheels were in motion. My parents and any family drama were far away, so many zip codes away, and I could breathe there." She smiled. "The park brought all of that back to me today."

Robert took it in, one of those lovely moments that arrive in treatment, when patients are happy. He thought of the celebrated denizens of Washington Square Park in other eras and how Kara had felt as free in the park as they did in their time: the Beats, the folk singers, the playwrights, the communists.

The session ended and Kara bounded out.

She stopped in the lobby and looked back guiltily at Robert's door. She'd neglected to tell him what really happened; that her mood that day wasn't just from visiting the park and remembering her freshman year, but from a potential new love story. For before the session, Kara had sat in the park and read the missive she'd received from her colleague, Sean, the one Jack had told her to sleep with.

She'd need to tell Robert about him and she would. But Robert had known Jack. She wondered if he might judge her, or if he might think that loving Sean would be shameful.

She mused: Though Jack wouldn't have minded, would he?

◻ ◻ ◻

Sean had been Jack's protégé at the firm, and he'd shown all the promise of an actual son. He'd transferred to Los Angeles for his wife's new job, she'd died in a car accident, and he'd moved back. By then, Kara had joined the firm.

Sean visited Jack at home, where he'd regale him with legal gossip and give him updates on his cases, but then Jack was reeling from the chemo and he told Sean not to visit anymore.

Sean would ask Kara about Jack, and they struck up a friendship. They both knew that Jack was on his way out. She was terrified, and she found comfort in Sean's understanding and experience.

Jack rallied, and he'd sit in the living room and ask Kara about Sean. And it was then that Jack started his "I'm a '60s guy" campaign, and said, "If you were with Sean, I wouldn't mind."

She'd get home from work and he'd ask, "Did you see Sean? How'd it go?" and she was alarmed to feel she was being too slow to commit the infidelity that Jack was waiting for.

She told this to Robert in their next session and she said, "That's when I insisted that Jack see a therapist and we found your name. I told you, I slept with one of my old boyfriends while Jack was still alive. In my mind, I was taking Jack up on his offer, and I just substituted Dan for Sean." She smiled. "I didn't even feel bad about it. It was as if I had permission."

"What happened?" Robert said.

"I'd go out nights, and I ran into Dan when I was at dinner with two of my girlfriends. We'd been together for a few years, after my divorce. He was a lawyer, as my husband was—do I only date lawyers?" she said and smiled. "We weren't able to make it last. We'd fight and we both said things we couldn't take back. What did I say? That I didn't think any woman would ever want to stay with him, stuff like that. Anyway, I passed him on my way to the bathroom. I told him to meet me at the bar at eleven, after I finished dinner. You know, Robert, he was safe and he didn't matter, so I had sex with him.

"As for Sean, well, we were becoming fond of each other and it seemed deeper than being lovers could possibly be. I knew he wouldn't have been up for a relationship so soon after his wife's death and, anyway, Jack was still alive, so I wouldn't have, either." She smiled sadly. "We used to cry to each other. It was a running joke between us. Two sad people. I was thinking about Jack and he was thinking about Jack, too, and about his wife, of course."

Kara stared at Robert for a moment and continued. "Back then, I knew that whatever might have been in the cards for Sean and me, it wasn't time yet; that any man I'd sleep with while Jack was still alive would be transitional, corrupted.

"Jack got worse, and Sean and I came to feel that any connection between us, even a friendship, was over the line, so we cut off all contact," she said. "Then Jack died ... Sean came to the funeral and we hugged. Then, what? A year of awkward contact in the office, until last week. He sent me this email."

She took out her phone and handed it to Robert.

He read:

Kara,
It's been a while. I've had time to think and I assume you have, too. Dinner next week?

"Oh," Robert said. "I see."

"He wants to meet and I'm fine with that. But we're just friends. Do you think he has more in mind?"

"What are your expectations?" Robert said.

"About Sean and me?" She thought a moment. "It would be inappropriate for me to be with Sean that way. It's still too soon for both of us."

"OK. Then don't," Robert said.

"Right, I won't."

On Saturday night, Kara was alone.

She cooked herself chicken with asparagus, and she opened a bottle of Burgundy. Kara thought of Sean while she ate but, after a second glass of wine, her thoughts drifted to Jack. She pulled out the red journal she'd given him. Jack had only written on one page. She smiled. He'd done it for her.

She read, again, how he never felt loved by the women in his life. Not by his mother, not by his first wife, Eleanor, nor by her. She put her hand to her stomach to keep from getting sick. Are men really that pathetic that they don't know when they're loved? she thought. And Jack? Couldn't he feel how much I loved him?

Then her mind flickered to a new thought: Put the journal away right now. And that became, throw it away, out the window. But she couldn't think of a rational reason for those thoughts, and who throws a journal out the window after drinking half a bottle of red wine? She didn't feel like moving.

She steeled herself and leafed through the empty pages. He'd only written on the one page, or so she thought, but then she saw more writing, another entry, pen on the page. It was just a few lines in a lonely spot near the back of the book.

How have I never noticed this before?

Kara looked away and took a deep breath. She didn't want to read it, but then she gazed back down. She saw that the page was dated the previous June.

When was that? she thought. Was Jack in remission?

Yes.

And then she read it.

Jack had written,

Kara and Sean, a perfect match? <u>They shouldn't be.</u>
<u>It's not right.</u>

She let out a yell.

Then Kara held her breath, looked up and tried to make herself, and the book, disappear. She stared at the framed photographs on her living room wall, her eyes resting on the elongated tulips in black and white, the flowers continuing in one frame where they left off from the previous one, but her gaze slowly drifted down to the Parsons table beneath the photographs, and then to the kilim rug, and then to her lap and the journal. Finally, she looked up. Her phone lay on a table across the room. It was like an alien. She stared at it and waited.

Ten seconds.

Twenty.

She slowly rose, walked over to it and picked it up.

She texted Sean: "I need to see you tomorrow."

They met the next day in Washington Square Park.

Before either could speak, Kara kissed Sean on the lips. He looked at her quizzically. She kissed him again and he responded with a short kiss. She kissed him a third time; he responded passionately.

"Come with me," she said.

Kara led him to a hotel on Waverly Place. They took a room and had sex, desperately and with yearning.

In their next session, Robert said, "Any news on Sean?"

"I met with him."

"Oh?"

"Yes," Kara said blankly. "It went fine."

"Fine?"

"Yes, fine," she said. She wanted to explain but then she stopped herself.

"Is there anything wrong?" Robert said.

She shook her head no, and she left.

Robert thought, That was strange but I'm sure she'll eventually fill me in.

After the session, Kara headed back to the park.

She didn't go in as she usually would but stopped under the arch. She noted some students sitting on the lip of the fountain. Then she closed her eyes and her mind turned to her husband.

… Hey, '60s guy! she thought, and she winced and smiled at what a throwback he was, his references so much older.

I'm sorry it was all so hard for you, Jack. You wanted to be my last love, didn't you? But I can't give you that. I just can't. Life's too long.

But I also know you didn't want me to love Sean, did you? You saw what it was and wanted me to kill it? To have us sleep together too soon, Jack?

That, I did. That I can give you, Jack, honey …

She opened her eyes. A female tourist was staring at her. Kara took out a mirror and a handkerchief from her handbag and wiped her face.

She stood under the arch for a moment longer and watched two NYU students who were talking by the fountain. The guy was gesticulating, apparently trying to keep the girl's attention, and the girl was smiling, her black hair blowing across her face.

Kara turned away from them and away from Washington Square Park for the last time. Then she headed north up Fifth Avenue, back into the city.

THE SADISM OF RED AND WHITE

(Jen)

I

Jen told Robert, her therapist, "I have big news."

"Yes?" Robert said, shifting in his chair. She'd entered therapy to address her relationships with men. They'd been working together for three years and Jen's news, usually male-related, often felt to Robert like an assault.

"I'm going to break up with Jacob tonight," she said.

"Oh?"

"Yes. We're going to dinner at Blue Hill and I'll probably even flirt with him there. Why, Robert? Well, you know how men get when I break up. Crying. Yelling. So I have to leave him wanting more, as in 'If you change a little we can try again in a few months' or 'Jacob, I just need a little space, then we'll see.' It will be our one-year anniversary."

Robert nodded and, a red wine drinker, thought ahead to the scotch with one big ice cube he'd have that night after the session. This made him smile, for Jen amused him. She also wore him out, yes, but he believed that getting worn out was part of being a therapist, and part of life itself.

Robert wasn't a masochist, though he sometimes felt like one in sessions—but Jen was a sadist, that was clear to him. He also knew that he was the most consistent person in her life; that they modeled, in therapy, what a healthy relationship might look like—which she yearned for in real life. He saw his progress with her as slow and steady.

Robert felt he could endure almost anything from her, and this was even easier because, well, he liked her. He had almost-boundless empathy for Jen. Where did it come from? Perhaps from the day she told him that being of mixed race, Japanese and Swedish, she didn't look like either of her parents, "so I've always been alone." Or when he learned that her father left the family when she was only nine. She never said anything about it except "it ruined me."

It was because of one of those, surely ...

Jen would often text him on her way to the sessions— "I hope you're ready! I'm going to be a lot today!"—clearly aware that her emotional weight might be a burden to him. Robert felt this was an open question in Jen's life: *Can anyone deal with me?*

He understood the I'm-on-route texts as her trying to take care of him, a nod toward reciprocity, and he'd text back, "I'm ready for you! Don't worry!"

Jen also brought him gifts on two occasions: once wildflowers; another time, a book by Alan Watts, *Becoming Who You Are*. "Philosophical tips?" he'd asked, and she'd smiled and said, "A loaner. I'm reading it, I thought you might like it." Though gifts were not quite allowed, he didn't mind those. He felt, deep down, she wasn't flirting. He sensed, instead, that she was looking for him to help her and didn't want him to give up on her.

He never would.

She'll experience a healthy connection with me, he often thought ... My stability is stronger than anything she might throw my way.

Jen was facing him in one of the two large chairs, waiting for him to talk, but he was recalling the time—when was it, a year and a half back?—when she'd broken up with her previous boyfriend, Charles, the one before Jacob. Yes, that's when it was, a year and a half before.

She'd told him about it in session.

"Do you know what I discovered, Robert?" she'd begun.

"What?"

"Charles has been keeping emails that his ex, Heather, sent him. Can you imagine?"

Robert remembered it all.

She'd stared at him for a moment and continued. "I said, 'I'm stunned by this, Charles, but I think we can start fresh if you'll just delete them,' and he did, Robert. But when he handed me the phone, I saw that the emails were still in his trash. I didn't want Charles, on some lonely night, to be able to read them again, ever. So I had him delete them from the trash, too. Then I initiated sex and faked a neighbors'-noise-complaint-level orgasm." She paused. "In the morning, I made him his favorite breakfast: eggs, sausage, with a chicory coffee from La Colombe, 'La Louisiane.'" (Robert remembered the name because he'd tried it after the session. It was delightful coffee.) "I kissed him goodbye at the door, and then I blocked him and never spoke to him again." She wore the trace of a smile.

□ □ □

Jen had discarded Charles and here they were, a year and a half later, and she was planning to break up with her current boyfriend, Jacob.

Robert asked himself if it were even worthwhile to put in his two cents, but he knew he had to.

"Jen?"

"Yes?"

"Last year Jacob kissed Kate on the lips at Thanksgiving," her sister. "You claimed it didn't bother you, but you've brought it up week after week. If that's why you're angry at him, why not confront him instead of breaking up with him? Tell him."

"Never."

"How did you put it? He had his hand on the small of her back and he drew her in."

"Exactly!" Jen said. "He had his hand on the small of her back and he drew her in."

They'd repeated the phrase so often in their sessions that Robert was like a trained parrot. For the rest of his life if anyone said, in film or on TV, "the small of the back," he'd involuntarily complete the sentence. "He drew her in?" Robert said. "What does that even mean? A momentary hug?"

"We've discussed this, Robert. A Thanksgiving kiss should be on the cheek, or both cheeks if we're Euro wannabes. His hand was on the small of Kate's back—"

"Yes. I know."

He looked at her and remembered that Kate had once stolen Jen's boyfriend, back when the girls were in high school. The sisters didn't speak for months and their mother had eventually officiated. But that was long past. He knew that Kate had spent years apologizing and, since high school, was always respectful around Jen's boyfriends. Robert also took Jen at her word that she'd forgiven Kate: they texted daily and visited each other twice a year. Kate lived in Massachusetts.

But if Jen didn't blame Kate, the same could not be said about men in general. She didn't trust men, and Robert knew that one day she'd likely feel she didn't trust him, either. That was to be expected and would be valuable; they'd work it through. He thought, Jen will be able to decide if men—or at least one man—can be in her corner.

Still, from the way she held his gaze, as she was doing just then, Robert felt the responsibility of his position. And, yes, once in a while, Jen made him nervous.

□ □ □

Robert permitted himself *nervous*.

Though psychotherapeutic patients expected their therapists not to have reactions or flaws, Robert and his colleagues had them—and so, were human.

In his training, Robert had been taught to play to his patients' illusions. The transference was everything: his patients needed to be free to imagine that he was whomever they needed him to be.

That was likely a productive idea, but Robert found the psychological orthodoxy to be, for him, unbearable and a bit ridiculous. He harbored a secret theory: hiding himself would lead to his eventually feeling alienated from his patients. He loved the work and didn't want to "protect the village by burning it down."

So he was anything but a wallflower. He didn't make a point of revealing too much—but wasn't afraid to show his patients who he really was, when it was relevant. In so doing, if he occasionally let slip a less-than-flattering anecdote about himself, he expected his patients to deal with that, too.

Confident that he was a good guide and that he'd helped so many of them—as they'd let him know over the years—he expected, in return, that they'd understand that the one who was helping them was not *other*, not merely existing in their minds, but was real. Exceedingly so.

□ □ □

He looked at Jen.

Where were they?

She was going to break up with her boyfriend, Jacob, on their one-year anniversary. Robert brought his attention back from his thoughts and her past.

"You know, Robert," she said. "I asked Kate about Jacob kissing her at Thanksgiving. She was upset that I brought it up again." Jen laughed. "Do you know what she said?"

"What?"

"'He was on the line, but he was drunk and he's not that guy, Jen.'" She rolled her eyes. "Kate said, 'You accuse every one of your boyfriends of doing things they don't do.' That's probably true." Jen shrugged and smiled. "I guess I have a problem. But I want Jacob to think of me after I leave him."

"How so?" Robert said.

She sat back. "I imagine him going to Joe's on Waverly Place for coffee. He goes most mornings. But after the breakup he won't say 'the usual,' a macchiato, but he'll be thinking my name first, and the barista won't suspect it. For months, years, not 'Should I take the subway or a cab?' or 'Should I wear a tie?' but my name, 'Jen, should I take the subway or a cab?' But I won't be there."

"That's the plan?" Robert said, and Jen nodded.

"What does that do for you?" he said. She didn't answer.

Robert took a deep breath. "OK, Jen," he said. "Your boyfriends become infatuated with you, and that's what you crave, yes? And from what you've told me of Jacob, he feels the same."

"He does?"

"I can think of ten events from the past year that speak to that," Robert said.

"Name them," she said.

"He left you flowers outside your door at least twice, right? That's two," he said. "The weekend you spent in the Adirondacks for your birthday and the toast he made at dinner—"

"All right, Robert. Stop."

"My point is this: Jacob's crazy about you," he said. "But here's the thing: you only have proof of this with men, in your own mind and imagination, when you leave them. You only seek proof of this by leaving them. Then you imagine that they think of you."

Jen looked at him, wide-eyed, "I told you. Kate—"

"Right. He had his hand on the small of her back and he drew her in, Jen, but hear what I'm saying. The real art is letting them be beguiled by you while you stay rather than when you leave," he said. "Do you think you can do that? Is that a goal? Can you try it with Jacob?"

Jen's mind was reeling. She stared at Robert and thought, Whatever. I don't need to speak.

Then she looked away from him and went off into her own world.

Here is this man, my therapist, she thought, and he's waiting for me to change. He's a captive audience, I'm paying him, and I can come back next week or never come back at all. It's up to me.

She thought how her father still sent her birthday cards every year and hoped for anything, even a smoke signal, in return ... And it's up to me with him as well.

She thought, Why did I seek therapy in the first place? Robert can't possibly understand who I really am and I won't show him that, anyway.

It's too ugly.

She found herself looking at him and nodding her head.

Yes, this is why I'm here. It's in Robert's eyes and his expectant face, in his waiting, always waiting. He'll wait for me for years if I want him to. His attention is better than Charles's was, or even Jacob's. The feeling is, yes, sensual, the way he looks at me and waits for me to unburden myself in the sessions.

Do I want to have sex with him? No, he's too old, ten years is my limit, fifteen tops. But I love his yearning and his desire to be there for me.

She thought of her journal and she made a mental note to record the idea: a little corner of the world is there for me.

... And anyway, I can yell at him, seduce him, or leave him, whatever I want.

She brought her attention back to the room and smiled. She loved making the world wait, and wait some more. The session was ending and Robert was staring at her; he looked bewildered.

She said, "Time to stop," and she rose and left.

Outside in the street, Jen's contentment faded. As she lifted her arm to hail a cab, she thought of an image from a French novel she'd studied at Barnard. The remembered section of the book stopped her in her tracks. For if therapy was one template—a kind of kitsch *let's heal!* situation—the scene from the novel was reminiscent of something else altogether, a more troubling aspect of who she really was. She knew that it could eviscerate her ability to ever again work with Robert.

She quickly put it out of her mind.

□ □ □

Jen met Jacob that evening at Blue Hill for their anniversary.

At first sight, from the way he smiled and kissed her hello, she could see how much he loved her. She didn't know what to do with that. His affection seemed to be too precious.

They had martinis at the table and Jacob made a toast to "one year and counting," but then they had little to say, and they ate their entrees in silence. How frustrating, she thought. Her mood picked up when Jacob put his hand on her leg. She was wearing thigh-high stockings and he ran his hand onto her knee, then higher. As his finger passed the top edge of the seam and moved to her soft upper thigh, he smiled. She looked at him, raised her eyebrows and smiled back.

They'd come to the same restaurant on their first date a year before, and they knew it was where Barack Obama had recently taken Michelle for dinner. The president and the first lady had flown to New York on Air Force One. Jen remembered the photo in the *Post* the next day. The Obamas looked dashing on Washington Place, he in a white shirt, dark pants, and a blue blazer, and Michelle in her glittering black dress. They were backlit by the street lamps, and there were Secret Service snipers above them, unseen, on the stately townhouse roofs.

A year before the sommelier had said, "They sat at your table."

During that first date, Jacob also put his hand on Jen's leg and he'd moved his hand up higher, past the top of her stocking to her thigh. His touch hadn't excited her the first time, though she'd enjoyed his boldness. Yet now, on their last night as a couple, she was turned on—though she knew that his hand wouldn't venture high enough to realize.

Watching him, she thought that every time they were together, Jacob's love seemed to grow. An early touch on her thigh and now the same a year later. Jen noticed his eyes moisten. She wondered if that was the problem: His passion was different from hers. She wasn't affectionate.

She finished her steak, he finished his salmon, the busboy cleared the table and the waitress approached. "Some dessert?" she said.

Jen watched Jacob's eyes shine as he looked at the waitress. She noted that he smiled at women in general; he seemed to regard them as his own personal harem—though he'd never cheated, not as far as she knew.

"We have a frozen hazelnut parfait, with Argyle Farms maple yogurt mousse, espresso syrup, and warm grappa candied chestnuts," the waitress said.

"Interesting," Jacob said.

Was it really? Jen thought. It's just a dessert, for Christ's sake.

The waitress rattled on as her boyfriend watched her, rapt. Jen assumed that he was noticing the effects of the waitress's push-up bra under her blue button-down shirt.

Jacob thought about his choices and then he decided: "The caramelized pineapple, with sauterne zabaglione, and grapefruit marmellata, with two spoons."

Jen considered how she'd break up with him.

After the meal. That would be best. So there it is, she thought. I have a plan.

They ate the dessert in silence, and then Jacob said, "Would you like an after-dinner drink?"

"No, we should get going," Jen said in a furtive whisper, a promise of things to come.

He settled the bill and as he held her coat, she thought, I'll wait. I'll let him take me home and tell him there, at my front door.

They walked outside to the street and she knew that this would be a violent act. She briefly wondered what Robert would think, and if he could even imagine who she really was.

And with that, she remembered the French novel that she'd tried to forget.

II

It was *Un Roi Sans Divertissement* by Jean Giono. It took place in Manosque, a village in the foothills of the Alps.

In the winter of the story, it had snowed for weeks on end. The town was blanketed by an oppressive white covering, which blocked out all signs of life. It was too thick to shovel or move, and the townspeople, mostly farmers, could only wait and endure the oppressive boredom of being shut-in and the excruciating monotony of their frozen world. The whiteness was glaring in the sun and visible as a sheet in the moonlight.

That winter, the townspeople were in the midst of a crime spree of a horrific sort: a man was slaughtering their farm animals. Or seemingly slaughtering them, because the animals were being abducted. The only evidence of the crime, apart from the animals' absence, was the red blood the villagers found on the white snow outside their barns. And oddly, after the initial shock, when they were too tired to focus on their loss and the moral depravity of the crime, through bleary eyes and despite themselves, they became transfixed by the sight, the break from the chromatic monotony: red blood on white snow. It was visually captivating.

Her professor had explained that it was as if the criminal found the white blandness as stultifying as they all did and, an artist unconcerned with petty morality and only wanting to please himself and make something beautiful, he turned this white canvas fiery, dramatic, the color of the heart.

As Jen walked to her apartment holding Jacob's arm, she thought of Robert's premise: that she wanted to beguile men but only felt the proof of it by leaving them. She tried to imagine what Robert would say in the next session. She wondered what he might have in his little bag of tricks. My Lord, she thought, will I be expected to pontificate about dear old Dad, as if his behavior led to this moment? As if I were merely a puzzle that could be deconstructed, reconstructed, and would yield a perfect result: a satisfactory, loving relationship? Cue the cymbals, cue the horns.

She smiled to herself on West 4th Street, thinking how she'd play along in the next session. Perhaps she'd even dig up an old memory of her father. But what Robert could never know was something else entirely. What if life happened the other way around? Or at least, what if it did for her? What if she wasn't lost at sea, a damaged soul, but a proud one? And if the act of rejecting her boyfriends didn't arise from the events of her past, not from what her father did, or Charles did, or anyone else?

In other words, this: What if she dumped these men because, well, she really enjoyed doing so?

She thought of how in the novel, the villagers, haunted by the crime, wouldn't get lost in the why of the act. Whether it was because the criminal's father beat him or his mother hated him. Interpretation would be an insult to the moment. No, better put, interpretation would be an insult to the art, to the criminal's pleasure in putting red on white.

Pain was more intimate than pleasure. Jen wasn't about to tell Robert that a man's face, at the moment of rejection, was more candid and true than that same face in the grips of an orgasm. It was riveting. But that was none of Robert's business. Not yet.

She asked herself one last logistical question as they turned onto Jones Street. Would she let Jacob kiss her before she delivered the news?

They climbed the stairs of her front stoop.

"May I come in?" Jacob said.

"Hmm," she said, and she stared into his eyes. She knew that in her hesitation, he'd kiss her.

And yes, she allowed him one long kiss.

□ □ □

She sat in her next session with Robert.

"I broke up with Jacob," she said.

"How do you feel about that?"

"Fine," she said blankly.

Robert stared at her and she smiled.

He thought, This will take some time but I'm sorry, my friend, I have all the time in the world ... We'll break through, eventually.

And Jen was looking at him. She found the idea of being potentially helped by this older man quaint and endearing. She met Robert's eyes and watched him.

Then she looked away and let him wait.

And wait some more.

SIRENS

(David)

David was wearing a sports jacket, a blue button-down shirt, dress pants and polished black shoes when he came to Robert's office for the first time. He waited at Robert's open door and smiled shyly.

"Are you ready?" he said. "Is it the right time?"

"Of course," Robert said. "Come in."

David walked into the office and they shook hands. Then he took off his sports jacket, placed it on the sofa and sat in one of the big leather chairs.

There was a moment of awkward silence and Robert said, "What brings you to treatment?"

"Should I just start in?"

"Sure."

"That's why I'm here, I guess," David said, smiling nervously, and Robert nodded.

"OK, so: I was happy in my life," he said. "I work in banking but I haven't gone to work in two weeks. I'm thinking of quitting and my brother suggested that I come to see you."

"What happened?" Robert said.

"You know how you can have an aquarium and put a drop of ink in it, and it all turns dark? That's what happened."

"How so?"

"I went to Amsterdam two months ago. I was traveling alone and I picked up a woman in Dam Square. Do you know Amsterdam?"

"No."

"Let me ask you this: Do you think a person can be an illusion?"

"In what way?" Robert said.

"I mean she was real. I really met her. I really slept with her. But now I think that in some way she's not real at all."

"Why don't you tell me what happened?"

David sat back in his chair. "I'm in the real estate department of a bank," he began. "I had a few weeks before my job began, so I traveled. I thought it would be my last gasp of freedom before I started working; my first job after college. I saw this girl, Danielle, in the Van Gogh Museum.

"I'm awkward with women. Maybe that's part of why I'm here. I don't know what to say to them or what to do with them," he continued. "We stared at each other for a minute or two. I thought she was interested in me but I couldn't tell. Perhaps she was trying to encourage me, I don't know. But I left and I saw her later that afternoon in Dam Square. There's a monument in the center, a pillar, and she was sitting on the circular steps surrounding it. We recognized each other from the museum. And unlike me, unlike who

I am because I'm very shy with women, I walked right up to her, she was sitting between her two girlfriends, and I talked to her. I don't remember what I said. I had a sense that she wasn't American. It was a how are you?-type thing, but she made it easy and asked me some questions. It just flowed and it worked, somehow ...

"Maybe it became easier because she told me she was from the South of France. I've never been there but I've always dreamed about it. I guess we all do," David said, and he tilted his head to a Monet print on the wall.

Robert nodded. He had a reproduction of Monet's *Poppies at Argenteuil* in his office. It depicted a nineteenth-century woman and a young girl walking through a field of red poppies. The woman carries a parapluie, the day is overcast, and the painting has an overall melancholic cast. Unlike the original art on his walls by contemporary New York artists, Robert always felt that the Impressionist reproduction didn't belong. He'd taken it with him—loaned it to himself, is how he put it— from the office where he'd done his residency, a sentimental holdover from those early years. Yet he was still moved by the exploding red dots and dashes from Monet's paintbrush. Robert always thought of the field as being sprinkled with red poppies; littered with them. And David had taken note.

"I'd rented a bicycle and I invited her, Danielle's her name, to take a ride. Again, not as I'd normally do," he continued. "She climbed on and as I pedaled away, she put her head on my back. I turned around at a light, I kissed her and, well, we ended up spending the night ...

"It was amazing. I remember us in bed, Danielle on top. I looked up at her face. I was in a dream state; I had my hands on her hips and I was thinking: She has French lips. They were pursed, made to say the *je's, veux's, peux's*; I took French in high school. Not lips for the hey-dude American vernacular. Crazy, right?"

David looked to be far away and then he continued, more slowly, "It was like being in a movie and I was the lead, the man who could be Danielle's boyfriend and lover.

"But now it seems like make-believe. Because it was just that one night," he said. "We dressed and went out. We held hands and walked through Amsterdam's red-light district, that tourist area. All of the prostitutes were behind the plate-glass storefronts like three-dimensional mannequins, but slutty and rough. And they looked at us. Danielle has bangs, high cheekbones, she wore an olive-green T-shirt and jeans, but her clothes fit differently from the way I see people's clothes fitting here. At least I thought so. Can a T-shirt be cut differently? Tighter? I don't know." He laughed. "The point is: For that moment, that day, I was the man with this incredible woman. That's who I was. She was my age but she seemed older. And passing the prostitutes behind the plate-glass windows, we huddled against each other; we had something they didn't have, and that was going to be it for us. We were going to be together."

David stopped talking and he cried. He reached for a tissue on the side table, wiped his face and said, "We went back to the hotel and got back into bed."

He took a moment, remembering.

"The next morning, Danielle left Amsterdam. Just like that. She traveled with her girlfriends to Denmark," he said. "I didn't think to stop her because it felt like it was unfolding in a movie and I was just one of the characters. Do you understand? It was like destiny. I'd slept with this girl from the South of France, and we were supposed to be together, that was obvious, and then she was leaving. It was so big a shift, so fast. Because the first part of the story, that we met at all, was improbable, and less than twenty-four hours later, the second part, my standing in the street waving goodbye at a white Volkswagen with three women in it, with Danielle crying and waving from the back window, was no less improbable. It was normal to let them drive away, not to yell 'Stop.' We'd barely begun and it was over …

"I came back and went to work. I'm in the real estate department of a bank, as I said. It's what I do and what I want to do. We fund skyscrapers and large architectural projects. But they started me in the appraisal department and that's where I am now. So this is my day, every day: I drive with this old Irish guy through Brooklyn and Queens, and we determine the value of houses for people who've applied for loans. It's a temporary position. But let me tell you, the contrast between that and having been Danielle's boyfriend—or whatever I was—is unfathomable," he said. "Those twenty-four hours in Amsterdam can't possibly transfer to New York. I don't have enough money to live alone, so I couldn't bring Danielle to live here. And how would she fit in here, anyway?

"So I thought, OK, Amsterdam was a moment in time and this is the real world. She's not a part of it and I'll just let it go, the way you'd let a dream go. It's over, right? But then she sent me a letter. Snail mail. May I read it to you?"

"Sure," Robert said.

David slowly took out a sheet of blue paper that made a soft, pliant sound, like tissue paper. He held it up so Robert could see an attractive blue script. He said, "She uses blue fountain pen. It's really too much."

He read:

David, I worry about you meeting another girl who would make you forget me and turn to this silly life most men have, always running, hiding, counting, buying, drinking, smoking, and losing his smile for a wife who believes that life goes no further than herself.

David carefully put the letter back in his pocket. He and Robert sat staring at each other, two men and the invisible presence of a phantom woman from the South of France.

Robert was happily married.

He remembered the day he met his wife, Marianna. A mutual friend had broached the idea of introducing them but it took him two years to get around to it. On that day, a Saturday in July, Andy and Robert arrived outside Island, a restaurant on the Upper East Side. Marianna was having lunch there with a girlfriend. The plan was that she'd come out at two o'clock, and the three of them would get coffee and dessert. He and Andy chatted on the sidewalk and waited.

At exactly two, Marianna took a step outside but she didn't let go of the door. Robert saw that she was beautiful. She smiled at him and held up five fingers to indicate she'd be five minutes late, with a faux wince. Then she went back in.

Robert liked her right away. It was about the smile, the hand gesture and the wince. In mere seconds, she'd communicated that she was considerate; she cared about others and their time.

His feeling for her never changed from what was formed in that first instant. Though liking her grew into loving her, deeply and passionately, there always remained that essential element that took root outside Island. In treatment with so many of his patients, Robert had come to understand that in any relationship, like mattered as much as love. He'd seen so many couples break up who still loved each other but couldn't stand each other.

Yet in hearing of David's letter from Danielle, Robert instantly understood David's predicament as if it were his, too, as if the letter had dropped a spot of black ink into his own clear tank of water. It was apparently cast in the same form in which Marianna had originally presented herself: in the letter, Danielle was thinking about David's welfare, not her own.

"I don't want you to be like those other men."

What had she written?

"The silly life most men have."

He wondered if he was just giving Danielle the benefit of the doubt? It was hard to tell. There was also the unknown X factor, the South of France. Robert asked himself: How could David's entry-level job compete? He thought, This guy's so together, he likes his career path, and then he met this incredible woman. Can he find a way to make it work for him here? Can't he have her join him, even if it would be difficult?

But no sooner had those thoughts passed through Robert's mind than David said, "I didn't read you the whole thing. At the end, she wrote this—" and he took the letter back out.

You can write back to me through the post office, David, but no texts, no emails, and no FaceTime. I won't answer those.

David stopped reading. "I tried to text her but she'd blocked my number."

Robert looked at him, his brow furrowed.

"For her, it was a one-off," David continued. "She doesn't want to see me again," and once more, David cried. Robert waited.

"I've stopped going to work," he said. "I've written her letters and I keep trying to contact her online, but she won't answer. Who is she? I need your help. Or, I need to get some balls, go to the South of France, and get her. But I don't know if that would work. I told you, I'm not that guy. I'm pretty shy with women. But why would she mail me that letter? Was I just a diversion for her?"

"I don't know why Danielle did what she did, David," Robert said.

David quietly said, "Where do we start, then?"

"I guess with how it's affecting you."

"I've been missing a lot of work."

"You stay home, you said?"

"I do, and I then go online and look for airfares to France, to Marseille. My boss gave me a warning yesterday."

"And you like this job, right?" Robert said.

"I like where it will take me."

"So, may I suggest that you go to work and we'll figure out the rest?" Robert said.

"You're telling me to go to work?" David said.

"Asking."

He could see that David was taking it in.

"All right," David said. "I will."

□ □ □

During the week that followed, Robert tried to recall Danielle's letter. What had she written to David?

I don't want you to be as most men are, "always running, hiding"—and Robert tried to remember the rest. He wondered if she were really as lovely a person as the letter implied, or if it were all a manipulation. And why wasn't she letting David call her? It struck Robert as a seduction. If they were on FaceTime or on the phone, she might lose her magic. Letter-writing left the space for David to imagine her, cherish her, and even experience her as some kind of goddess for being unreachable.

At the start of the next session, David said, "I haven't missed a day of work since last week," and Robert nodded. "It's depressing, though. I told you, I'm working with this old guy. He gets red in the face. Yammers on."

"What kind of work do you do?" Robert said.

"We drive around in this car, a Prius, and we appraise houses and buildings. Did I mention it? It's in anticipation of my being transferred to the office in a month or two.

"His name's Kevin," David continued. "He's taught me to look at houses as people. That's what he said. The walls are the skin and they're made of brick, block, stone or wood. The roof is like the top of the head, it's made of asphalt shingle but sometimes slate or tar paper. But houses are not people, Robert."

"No."

"But he did talk about one person, Judy Garland. Do you know her?"

"Yes," Robert said.

"Actress, singer, *The Wizard of Oz*. She died young from drugs and alcohol," David said.

Robert nodded.

"So Kevin turned to me in the car and he said, 'If Judy Garland hadn't been a star, she'd have lived much longer. She would have married well, a doctor.'" David looked at Robert and smiled. "Kevin said, 'It was celebrity that killed her. If she'd given it up, she'd probably have lived in Brooklyn, on Ocean Parkway. Her kids would have driven her crazy and she would have yelled at them before dinner, as everyone does. It wouldn't have been glamorous, but it would have been better for her than all of the drugs and all of the unhappiness.'"

David looked at Robert. "Judy Garland would have married well? Do you see what's happening here?" he said.

"What?" Robert said.

David's eyes became wet. "Contrast what Kevin said to me, to this. Another little friend arrived in the mail. May I?"

Robert nodded.

David took out a letter and read:

David chéri,
I stopped my bicycle on the side of the road by a field
of sunflowers (I don't think that anyone can say that
I can't take these vibrant flowers since they're part of
nature) and I cried and remembered our lovely time
in Amsterdam.

"It goes on, but contrast Danielle to, well, aspiring to being more basic. To Judy Garland living on Ocean Parkway," David said, and he looked at Robert. "I tried to call her again online. It bounced."

"Did you write?" Robert said.

"A short one. Mailed it at the post office, as instructed. I wrote that I loved her, missed her, didn't understand her-type thing. But I need to get over this. It's infuriating.

She's messing with me and I don't like it. Let's start there. I just don't like it. I don't know if I like her, frankly.

"You know, when we were in bed in Amsterdam, flowers came up. Flowers in the South of France," David continued. "I was blown away even then. The mystique. Maybe even then I was preparing myself for this, for Judy Garland on Ocean Parkway, instead of the woman with the bangs, the high cheekbones and the small breasts, in bed." David sank back into his chair. "Why do you think she's doing this to me?"

"I don't know, David," Robert said.

"So? Then?"

"So then we need to work on you, not her," Robert said. "What do her letters bring up for you?"

"She's taunting me. That I had her and I'll never have her again."

"So the letters suggest that her life is better than yours? That's what you implied. That she has flowers on the side of the road?"

"Yes," David said. He nodded toward the Monet on the wall. "It's really sad, that picture."

"I know," Robert said.

"I think you need to take it down."

"I was thinking that, too," Robert said and smiled. "But we all dream of that, right, David? Riding a bicycle and passing a field of poppies, as Danielle does in real life?"

"Right. You're my therapist. You didn't even know that I was coming and you have it on your wall. How do you explain that?"

"It's by Monet. It's his red dots and dashes that I like. If you could find the flowers here, in New York, then maybe Danielle wouldn't matter."

"But I can't find them here in New York. We don't have fields of poppies. Or fields of sunflowers. Or of lilacs."

Robert nodded. "Here's the thing, David. In our minds, memories become symbols and the whole trick of therapy—the whole trick of life, I think—involves manipulating symbols. They're more agile than memories. If we can change them, then the memories themselves change. If you can transform the present, it transforms the past."

Robert looked at David, saw his blank expression and thought, He didn't follow what I just said.

"Danielle and the flowers have taken on a symbolic value to you. What do you think they represent?" Robert said.

David thought for a moment. Then he said, "A better life in France. A worse one here, as you said before. If she can ride her bicycle by a field of flowers, then I've got nothing."

"So how about this? We turn this into a symbol of our own, you and I. We'll each look for the field of poppies."

"But it doesn't exist in New York," David said.

"No, but let's just open up the possibility, whatever that might mean to you. On the day either of us finds it, we'll notify the other. Deal?" Robert said.

"On the day either of us finds a field of poppies?"

"Yes."

"In New York?"

"Yes."

"It's a deal," David said.

Robert reached out his hand and they shook on it.

They were silent for a moment and then David said, "I want her to stop writing to me but I won't ask her to." Then he looked at the clock and Robert did. It was time to stop. "Any advice for the coming week?"

"Yes, David," Robert said. "Remember that you were the guy who initiated the contact with Danielle. You're that guy."

"Right. You know, I'm on the dating apps but I'm not interested. But I'm that guy. All right. I'll try to remember that."

David stood to go and Robert said, "And remember our deal. About the poppies."

□ □ □

In Aix en Provence, France, Danielle walked down the narrow streets, past the old stone facades of the buildings.

She was wearing an outfit that wasn't overly provocative, a sweater with a low V-neck, jeans, leather ankle boots and a blazer. Men were taking notice. She wasn't trying, but she was young and she knew that she didn't need to try. They passed her on the street and wanted to talk to her, to know her, and many, to have sex with her.

She pulled a letter to David out of her handbag and dropped it into the postbox.

□ □ □

When David came in for his next session, Robert said, "Did you find the flowers?"

"No," David said, as he sat down. "No fields speckled with red poppies or teaming with sunflowers in New York City."

"We have flower markets. There's one close, in Union Square," Robert said.

"You want me to stare at flowers in a flower market and pretend I'm in the South of France with a French woman, and to pretend she desires me?"

Robert shrugged.

"I was thinking of what you said, though," David continued. "That I was the guy who'd initiated the meeting. That meant something ... During the week I was trying to think of her less often. I know being with her that day in Amsterdam was a good—no, a remarkable—experience, but it's over. And I was thinking, if I can make it disappear, then I can do anything." He smiled. "But my world—Kevin at the bank—is conspiring to lead me to an ordinary life. Nothing special, nothing reminiscent of bedding a French girl in Amsterdam or a field of red poppies," and he gestured to the Monet on the wall.

"But you know, Kevin distracted me from thinking about Danielle this week," David continued.

"How did he do that?" Robert said.

"OK. So, we drive around the boroughs in the car from the bank. Remember?" he said. "And get this! We park in front of these houses or condos, usually in Brooklyn, sometimes in Queens or Staten Island. And

I noticed that Kevin gets out of the car, and he stops in the street and raises his nose, like a rabbit. He sniffs the air and says, 'Wood.' Or another time he said, 'Plastic.' I didn't put it together and then yesterday he clued me in on what it was."

"What?" Robert said.

"He was smelling fires, Robert. He'd sniff the air and say, 'Plastic, it must be industrial.' Or 'Wood. It's a frame house,' and within five minutes we'd hear the fire engines. Do you see? Kevin, the man who's training me, was a firefighter!"

"That's amazing," Robert said.

"He's retired. He smells the smoke and then we hear the far-off sirens."

David paused a moment.

"Yesterday Kevin told me about the job," David continued. "He said, 'They call to me.' He smells the smoke, hears the sirens, and yearns to speed over there to help the others fight the fires. I feel the same passion as he does, but it's wasted here," and he pulled out a blue crinkled missive from Danielle.

"So she's like a siren to you, David."

"What?"

"In Homer, the sirens called men to smash themselves on the rocks. You see?" Robert said. "Danielle lures your mind and imagination to think of her, to think of the fields of flowers, to colonize your attention and your life, to make you live in her dream."

David was staring at him, seeming to consider that, but his eyes teared up and he said, "I love Danielle. What'd you say again? Last week?"

"I said that you seduced her in Amsterdam and you'll be empowered again. You can do so many things, David. There's a lot in store for you."

Their next session was their final one before the summer break. David had booked a trip to Prague.

He looked at Robert and said, "We've only been doing this for a month, but I wonder how you think I'm doing? What do you think of me?"

What did Robert think of him or, more accurately, feel for him? In truth, tenderness. He reflected for a moment and he said, "I think you're smart and you have an original way of seeing things, David. You're not passive and that will be useful to you in life. And you're processing the Danielle affair in your own way. You'll move on when you're ready."

"Thank you," David said. "I'll see you in a few weeks"— and he tilted his head toward the Monet print—"as long as you get rid of that picture. It's too depressing."

"That's the plan," Robert said.

David traveled to Prague.

As he'd tell Robert, he found the Old Town Square to be unbearable, jammed with too many tourists. It was like Times Square at its worst, but then one night he went to the Hemingway Bar and that was better.

A woman stared at him from across the room. In her gaze, David felt like he was a force to be reckoned with. He stared back and wondered if he'd try to meet her. But then he thought, This would be like Danielle. If I were ever to do that again, I'd handle it differently. He looked at her and resolved, I'll talk to her if she comes over and talks to me.

But she didn't.

□ □ □

Neither David nor Robert would ever know what Danielle's life was really like. They couldn't possibly. Yet eight hundred and fifty miles from Prague, David's paramour from Amsterdam was alive and well.

Danielle took her place at the second of five desks in a flores- cent-lit, ground-level office in Aix en Provence. Her job was renting apartments to walk-ins. It was boring work and she knew she was underemployed.

In college, she'd been gifted at creative writing and chemistry, but when she graduated, she yearned to find a husband and have a family. She'd always thought, I'm just unambitious, lazy, really, but it was more than that— something deeper inside that colonized her motivations. It was Jean Claude's fault more than anyone's. He was her brother and he'd died when she was eight. Or maybe it was her father's fault; he'd reacted badly to his son's death, bien sûr, and pulled her to him in ways that weren't entirely sexual but were clearly over the line: holding her on his lap for too long, her legs straddling his knee, his arm around her undeveloped chest. She'd listen to his long confessions about how he couldn't talk to his wife about Jean Claude and needed to talk to her. This was beyond anything she could understand, but she was powerless to resist. She knew they were closer than her parents were to each other, and their talks, laden with her father's passion and tears, lasted into her early adolescence.

As a result, and despite her manifest strength as a woman, her childhood had rendered her a mere spectator in her present life. She couldn't completely grasp the precise definition of her paralysis but she sensed its power over her, and where it was leading her.

She took out a blue piece of stationery, like tissue paper, read what she'd written but, dissatisfied, crumpled it up.

Then she took out another piece of paper and her fountain pen and started again.

She wrote:

David,

I've been reading Virginia Woolf, and I think that perhaps men's opinions about women have never changed. The men I know dream of being in control. It makes me want to ask them (but I never do), Why do you fear women so much?

Take Marco. He had a girlfriend. I asked him if he loved her and he said yes, so I asked him why (dumb question, I know) and after hesitating, he said it's because she was refined and quiet.

Refined and quiet?

What I'd like to know is what these men find attractive in a girl who doesn't have her own life. Are men so self-satisfied that they only need to see themselves reflected in their women's faces?

If I were a man, I'd like a girl with her own point of view. I would get bored very quickly with the daily 'oui mon chéri'.

I go on ... but it bothers me.

I am thinking of you.

Je t'aime.

Danielle

She put it in an envelope.

In Amsterdam, Danielle had seen David in the Van Gogh Museum and stared at him. I can make him sleep with me with merely a regard, she'd thought. Yes, she'd have an affair with this—as she discovered when he spoke to her in Dam Square—American. A boy, not a man. On that day in Amsterdam, she felt herself to be a femme fatale; a seductress pour un jour. She'd have sex with a foreigner and wouldn't ever see him again.

He'll touch me everywhere, she thought, he'll kiss me everywhere. And he did. *I had him do that.*

Of course, marrying an American wasn't in the cards because she found them a bit ridiculous. A country that goes from Obama to Trump could never be serious. No, she'd marry French, but meeting David fed a fantasy that her life would be something more than mediocre, more than boring, more than trying to relate to men whom she couldn't stay with—because of what had transpired with her father. With David, she didn't have to truly connect. The entire *aventure* would only last a day.

She forbade him to call or text her after Amsterdam. Why waste time on something that had no future? Why risk that her future husband—and she had an idea of exactly who he was—would see an American boyfriend's texts on her phone?

But she did allow herself the indulgence of writing letters and they were a place for her to dream. To write to him about Provence and a world that may have existed in the twentieth century, or, say, for the fictional characters Colin or Chloe in *L'écume des Jours*, but didn't exist for her. She included in her letters her longings about life and relationships—she didn't think that David was a phallocrat like most of the men she knew—and they were a place for her to pretend that she was free.

She also included descriptions of flowers because, in Amsterdam, David had shown passionate interest in the fields of flowers near where she lived. So Danielle would describe the sunflowers and lilacs she'd cycle by every day outside Aix, on her way to work.

She omitted a description of the shopping center she passed near those fields, along the way.

Back at her desk, Danielle was bored. She knew that, worst-case scenario, she could do this type of unremarkable real estate work until she was sixty-two and then retire with full benefits—but she imagined she wouldn't be working for that long.

"I'm absurd," she thought, and she was always slightly depressed. She had hoped, when younger, for a life that would be guided by big loves, big risks, running away, passion, even suicide. She wondered if in her letters she was an obsession for David. Was he transfixed by her words? She hoped so because, well, it would match her own condition, the forces driving her in ways she couldn't control and couldn't escape, such as the man who was magnetically drawing her in.

Marco.

He'd been part of their friend group for a long time; she'd always found him to be insensitive and wild. But he'd asked her to go to a bar that evening after work, and she knew she'd go. She knew, deep down, that he was to be the one.

Marco, who smoked. Marco, who drank too much. "Not too much," Sylvie once said, "more than too much!" Marco, who was broken, having lost his sister as she'd lost her brother. He made grand displays of false spontaneity, which Danielle saw as recklessness—such as the time at a café when, to make a point in a philosophical conversation, he smiled and threw his chair into the street. It hit an oncoming car.

Her girlfriends warned that he'd never be able to sustain a relationship, let alone a marriage. But she knew that, yes, he would be hers.

She thought again of David. Her affair with him had checked off some boxes in her head. For that short time in Amsterdam, she hadn't been stuck, she'd seduced, and she'd been free.

She thought, Thank you, American boy. Keep dreaming.

She left the office and dropped the letter into the postbox.

□ □ □

Robert went to pick up his wife Marianna at the nail salon on 11th and University at dusk. There was a reception area with six chairs; beyond that, three reclining chairs for pedicures, and toward the back, eight tables for manicures. There was another level below, accessible by a spiral staircase.

The receptionist told Robert that his wife was on the lower level and instructed him to wait in the reception area. He sat down and gazed at his phone, but he was soon distracted by the powerful smell of nail polish wafting from the series of reclining chairs, where three women were getting pedicures. He tried to look back down and read the news, but the scent made it impossible to read. He'd get a headache.

Robert put his phone away.

He looked over and found the culprits of the smell. Ten wet toes painted vermillion, attached to an attractive, coifed, manicured, blond New York woman on her phone.

Her red toes reflected the light from the manicurist's lamp, glaring at him one after another, then together. They were annoying but they were reminding him of something, but of what?

He reflected how women's painted toenails elicited so much in him. First, there was the memory of his girlfriend decades before. One afternoon, she informed him she was ending their relationship and she proceeded to paint her toenails red. It had been shocking and when she did that, he understood that the impending breakup was real. For years afterward, Robert thought of women's painted toenails as evidence of their inherent egotism and arrogance.

But later in life, it all changed. Robert became a psycho-therapist and every summer Robert's female patients would arrive for treatment and their closed shoes and boots would give way to sandals. Robert never stared but he couldn't help but notice. The unexpected array of color would signify to him, every year, it's on. Whether at fifteen or fifty, Robert's seasonal awareness went from, will it ever be summer? to, it's here, we're in it deep in New York and we will be, brutally, for months. But summer always started gently and took him by surprise, his female patients heralding it in with an opening burst of levity and shine.

And then of course there was Marianna, his wife. She had frequent manicures and pedicures, and when they had dinner plans, as they did that evening, he'd wait for her in the front of the salon. Inevitably, often before bed, she'd ask how he liked the colors she'd chosen. Her choices varied with the seasons, burgundies in the winters and in the summers, mandarins, fuchsias, azures, and various other blues. Robert would repeatedly offer that he didn't like many of the blue shades; he found them unnatural. He was amused that she'd still ask him, like clockwork, what he thought of her color choices, while she remained completely indifferent to his input.

Then his mind came back to the moment. The salon and the aroma were evoking something, but he couldn't quite place what it was.

He thought of David and wondered how he was faring. Would he have an affair in Prague as he'd done in Amsterdam? Robert thought that would be healthy.

His mind wandered again, and he looked forward to dinner that evening. They'd be seeing old friends, Bill and Laura. She was a lawyer and Bill had intimated, by text, that she'd represented a British spy. Robert had read about it in the *Times* and he hoped that she'd tell them about the case. He smiled at the thought of it, Laura was an engaging story-teller—but then his smile faded. It was the dizzying odor again. It was too much. It was giving him a headache.

He looked at the woman to his right and now he saw, beyond her, two other women in the other reclining chairs, and his eyes went to their twenty toes, a field of floral flecks of color, in canary and lavender.

He thought of David again and then it came to him.

Yes! That was it!

He and David had shaken hands and pledged that they would tell each other when they'd found the field of poppies in New York City. A field spotted with them; littered with them.

He thought, David, I found it!

Robert reached for his phone but stopped himself. No, he couldn't text a patient on vacation; that would be a boundary violation, pathetic, and anyway, it was too small a thing.

He sat back and stared at the woman's ten red toes and the other women's twenty toes just beyond, and he closed his eyes.

Yes, David, he thought. It's here.

ILLUSION

Ghosts

The Ropes

When I was earning my degree, I interned with people afflicted with schizophrenia. It was a moving seven months of my life with those overwrought, pained clients, and I learned so much that I'd apply later on.

One encounter always stayed in my mind.

Jane was diminutive and in her sixties. Every day she'd sit in the lounge and she'd bury herself in the *New York Times*, which she'd read from cover to cover.

I was leading a group called Weekend Activities. On Fridays, I'd ask the eight or so participants to tell the group their plans for the upcoming weekend. People with schizophrenia tend to be socially reticent and it was useful for them to express themselves there.

One day Jane attended the group. She raised her hand and said, "What am I doing this weekend? It's going to be a hard one for me."

"Why?" I asked.

"This weekend is Mother's Day, and when I was young my children were taken away from me. They said that I wasn't mentally competent to raise them."

"I'm so sorry," I said.

"Even if they don't want to see me, if they'd just send a plant it would make me happy," and she added, without irony, "even if they'd send a cactus."

Then Jane turned away from the group and the discussion moved on. People's weekend plans were usually along the lines of walking in the park, getting ice cream at the local delicatessen, or watching a game show or a ballgame on TV.

After a few minutes, Jane turned back to the group and raised her hand. I called on her and she said, "You know, I'm aka Margaret Thatcher."

After giving the group a moment to let that sink in, she said, "I was very good friends with Ronald Reagan. Mahatma Gandhi once asked me to swim with him in the Ganges, but I refused. It's so polluted."

No one said anything.

Over the course of my internship, I noted how the others in the group and at the Day Center were always very tolerant of whatever ideas any of them came up with. I don't think they really believed that Jane had known President Reagan. I surmised that they generally suspected when someone was embellishing, or perhaps it sent many of them into their own imaginative swirls—but they never called each other out. Of course, as people who were medicated and suffering from schizophrenia, they were nonconfrontational by nature. But to me, their tolerance of each other's delusions and the generous, patient way they'd listen to each other's stories was an elegant aspect of their personalities; a kind of noblesse oblige.

□ □ □

My experience with Jane stayed with me.

The first thing about the story seemed so obvious. If a person's children were taken away from her because she wasn't mentally competent to raise them, it would tarnish her self-esteem. Perhaps such a person would walk with her head down or with slumped shoulders. But for Jane, with paranoid schizophrenia, what if those compensations would just be too little to do the trick? What if, instead of processing her shame, she had to transform herself into someone else altogether? A person of substance. Not the woman who was deemed mentally unfit to raise her kids but, say, a prime minister of England.

And of course, in dealing with a person afflicted with schizophrenia one couldn't say, "You're not Margaret Thatcher." Even as an intern I knew that she would have only thought that the CIA had sent me to confuse her about her true identity.

Yet in her reaction, Jane gave me a deeper understanding of people in general that I'd apply, later, in my practice.

Consider the patient I treated when I was a licensed psychotherapist, a money manager who invested a great deal of his holdings in oil. When the oil market crashed, he lost most of his fortune and had an affair, which would eventually lead to the dissolution of his marriage.

He didn't suffer from schizophrenia or from a personality disorder, and his mental machinations were more sophisticated than Jane's were but, I believe, ultimately not that different. To prove his competence in the face of defeat, he didn't need to say, "I'm really Warren Buffet, you know," and he didn't report to me that his lover said, "You lost money but, to me, you're as good as Warren Buffet," unlike Jane who went to: I'm really Margaret Thatcher. But he reported that his lover told him, "You're so handsome," and another time, "I feel alive when I'm with you," as compared to his wife, whom he'd said he imagined thinking, You're a nobody. You were too incompetent to play the market and win.

Jane couldn't bear being Jane anymore. And in a sense, this man couldn't bear being himself either——and his girlfriend showed him a different picture of himself from the one he saw reflected to him from his wife.

Jane compensated for her loss, and so did he.

□ □ □

But that patient wasn't the only one who told himself stories about himself, as Jane had.

I realized that I did, too.

A week after Jane revealed her misfortunes to the group, I remembered seeing her hunkered down in the lounge, reading the *New York Times*. Though I knew that the British Labor party was on the Left, I never quite knew who the Tories were, and as I recall, I walked up to Jane and asked her to tell me the difference between the two parties. She looked up from her newspaper and said, "The Tories are on the Right, Labor's on the Left," and I thanked her and walked away.

Over time, I patted myself on the back for that intervention. Knowing that Jane was highly literate, I'd found an authentic way to have her teach me something new. Yes, perhaps she even came away feeling, on some level, I'm not quite as much of a nobody. I'm not just the person whose children were taken away. I was also able to teach this man about British politics.

What a major score on my part!

Yet a few years later, looking back, I detected one little problem with my story.

I think I made it up.

I don't think it ever happened.

So what did happen?

Jane had told the group her children were taken away from her. Afterward, I'd walked past Jane in the lounge and I saw her reading the *New York Times*.

I felt very despondent and sorry for her. And I kept on walking.

And then?

Perhaps a year later, I must have remembered the situation and thought, Do you know what I should have done? I should have asked Jane to explain to me about the Labor Party and the Tories. And the idea of what I should have done and what I did—or more correctly, what I didn't do—became fused.

When I pieced it all together, I found the interesting point to be this: Wasn't my memory of how effective I'd been that day in the hallway by asking Jane about the Tory and Labor parties, well, wasn't it similar to what Jane had done with herself and Margaret Thatcher? Even a little?

I learned through this that many of our thoughts about ourselves are constructed to suit the circumstances. That's to say, we fictionally form our inner worlds. I don't think that is necessarily a bad thing, but I think it's good to know.

We live in the realm of storytelling and illusion.

□ □ □

As a therapist, I've seen how people get caught up in their fictional inner worlds. Those seem to be a primal aspect of who we are and how our minds work.

The next two stories are about illusions, the things we tell ourselves and what we go through to become fully alive.

As the other members of the Weekend Activities group did with Jane, we all tolerate the fictions of those around us but seem less aware of our own.

As Jane was. And the oil trader.

And as I was.

GHOSTS

(Sebastian, Jeremy)

I

Robert imagined an old man sitting on a park bench in Berlin. The year would be 1996. School children would run by and the old man, Sebastian, would hear their exuberant shouts but he'd look away and frown. To the passersby, he'd be typical, the type of older man who doesn't smile and who is consumed by his memories.

Robert once heard someone say that when one gets old, very old, the goal would be not to be pissed off all the time. That made him laugh. Another time he heard that the goal would be to try not to kick the local cats or dogs when no one was looking.

Still, Sebastian, the man in the park in Berlin, provided a strange contrast that afternoon.

The main question for everyone who would walk by would be: Can't he see how happy those children are? Can't he take in the beautiful day?

Stop thinking about Sebastian, Robert told himself. This is fictional, anyway. You're making him up.

Robert's new patient, Jeremy, rang the buzzer. It was time to go back to work.

He'd think about Sebastian later.

□ □ □

Jeremy came in, shook Robert's hand and settled in.

"I guess I should tell you what's going on and why I'm here," he said, and Robert nodded.

"Ten years ago, I married my wife, Emma. We met in high school on Long Island," he began. "I was kind of nerdy, she was a cool kid and she liked me. We were friends. Years later, we both took the train to New York every morning and we spotted each other on the platform. We started talking. One day she brought coffee and croissants for both of us. I asked her if she had weekend plans and we took it from there. It was a strong connection. She's an honest person and I appreciate that. But what I really liked was her integrity; I knew she'd never leave me. I need that type of security. But now I'm thinking of leaving her. I'm a bit ashamed to tell you that."

"What about your marriage dissatisfies you?" Robert said.

"I'm unhappy. You know, she's pretty. She's nice." He looked at Robert.

"I doubt you're thinking of leaving the marriage because of pretty and nice, are you?" Robert said.

"I was raised by my father," Jeremy said.

Robert leaned forward, and then Jeremy launched into his story.

When Jeremy's parents divorced, he was ten years old, and his father was granted custody of him; his mother of his younger twin sisters.

"I didn't know why my mother didn't want me. That's always been on my mind," he said.

Robert waited for Jeremy to say more, but he was silent.

"What do you remember about her from those early days?" Robert finally said.

"When I was ten, I'd sit on my bed in my father's house and I'd think of her," he said. "I only saw her on alternate weekends. I was in my little room and the house was empty. My father was working and my twin sisters lived with my mother. It was so depressing ... I'd think of the softness of her arms and her scent: it was gardenia. At the time, I thought she generated the scent herself. Years later, I realized that she wore gardenia perfume." He smiled. "... And she had a white cotton eyelet duvet cover. In my father's house, I'd think of it. It was crisp, freshly ironed and it smelled of lavender. The sun always seemed to strike it. I imagined I'd need sunglasses to gaze at that white cotton duvet in my mother's bedroom.

"And then there were the food scents," he continued. "Red sauce wafting through my mother's kitchen into the front hallway and upstairs. On my weekends there, I'd smell the aromas in the morning and try to imagine: Would dinner be spaghetti? Veal or chicken? Lasagna?"

Jeremy waited a moment and said, "My father's house was different. It was nothing to me. Do you know that I recently saw a photo of myself from that period? I was standing in front of the rose bushes just outside my father's living room window. Today, it's my sister Elizabeth's house, she lives there, and in the summer her living room is always filled with the scent of those roses. It must have been the same when I was growing up—but as a little boy, I didn't smell them. I think I went on a sensory strike in his house; roses didn't have an aroma. They weren't gardenia, lavender, red sauce," and he smiled and added, "or for that matter, Pledge or Clorox," and Robert understood: gardenia, lavender, red sauce, Pledge, Clorox, the olfactory palette of Jeremy's childhood longing.

"After the divorce, my father fought with my mother on the phone every night. I heard it all. He'd complain about money and alimony, and then he'd hang up and tell me 'She's crazy.' I think he once said, 'I don't know why you even see her.'

"He'd say 'She gets inside me.' Isn't that strange? I remember finding it disturbing at the time. I mean, men penetrate women, right? Or they penetrate men, whatever. But I often thought of that: in this case, women penetrating men. She was in him, in his mind, and making him go crazy. And making me go crazy; I knew she was in my mind, too. I couldn't stand seeing her only on alternate weekends.

"So one day I woke up and decided I'd had enough," he continued. "I was eleven by then. I didn't know why she didn't want me. You know, she expected me to survive on mere crumbs: weekend visits, memories of a duvet or the scent of red sauce. I needed to take a stand. I thought men did. I thought my father expected me to."

"What did you do?" Robert said.

"I stopped talking to my twin sisters. That was first," Jeremy said. "And then, just before one of our weekends together, my grandfather fell ill and my mother went to Dallas to see him. She canceled on me and I told her I didn't want to see her anymore. It hurt her badly, I could hear it in her voice and I liked that. My father defended my decision.

"There were a few memorable scenes after that." Jeremy smiled sadly. "She showed up at our front door and demanded that I come home with her on a Friday. I told her that I hated her. She physically pulled my arm, and I wriggled out of her grasp."

Jeremy removed a bottle of water from his briefcase and took a drink.

"It lasted a few years. I didn't speak to her. And then, eventually, I did. I started to go to her house again, but I never forgave her. I saw her sporadically for a few years, two or three, but then I stopped. That's why I'm here. I told you it was because of my marriage but it's really because of this."

"Because of what?"

"She's ill and she called me to go to see her. She has cancer. I wanted a backstop," Jeremy said.

Robert nodded.

They spent the last minutes of the session discussing the prospect of Jeremy returning his mother's call. Robert thought it was a good idea and Jeremy agreed. He decided he'd contact her and make a date to see her.

After the session, Robert thought of how people's lives became arrested in time and could sometimes be summed up in a single phrase. Jeremy had said: I didn't know why she didn't want me.

His mother didn't want him and now, presumably, his wife did, but it didn't count.

□ □ □

"I saw my mother," Jeremy said at the start of the next session, his eyes wet.

"How'd it go?"

"Wonderfully. I was in the hospital. We held hands," he said. "I felt close to her for the first time since I was nine years old,"

Robert smiled and said, "That's fantastic, Jeremy."

"She was in bed and we just sat there. We didn't talk much; it didn't seem necessary. We were just together."

He took out his water bottle and had a drink.

"I feel so different, Robert. Like I'm coming back to life. I tried to explain this to Emma. I told her about my mother. I think she knew the story, but this time I was really feeling it."

"How'd she react?"

"She was all in. Listening. Crying. She wants to meet my mother but I don't know," he said. "Our time is so limited. I'm going back to the hospital later today."

"Good. Jeremy," Robert said. "... Do you think there's anything you need to bring up with your mother?"

"What do you mean?"

"Well, you said to me, 'She didn't want me,'" Robert said.

"I should ask her about that? Really?"

"Not many people get the chance to."

"Oh."

"And as for Emma? She wanted to see your mother, but you don't think it's a good idea?"

"Do you?" Jeremy said.

"I don't know," Robert said.

Jeremy nodded. "She'd understand if I just want to spend time with my mother alone. My mother doesn't have long," and he added, "Emma's always there for me that way. I don't know what to do with it."

"With what?"

"Her affection. Do you remember I told you about the time my mother came to get me after I'd decided not to see her anymore? She was at the front door of my father's house, I was eleven, and I told her I wouldn't come out?"

"Yes."

"I've dreamed of that scene, but with Emma trying to get me to come out of the house and my saying no."

"Any thoughts about that?" Robert said.

"Not too many," he said. "If things are good with my mother, Robert, do you think I can start over with Emma, fresh? Do you think I can get my feelings for her back?"

"We can figure that one out," Robert said.

□ □ □

Robert's next meeting with Jeremy would end badly and cause Jeremy to take a break from therapy.

It started when Jeremy bounded in, upbeat.

"Fasten your seat belt!" he said. "I saw my mother and I did what you suggested … So, I was there for an hour. We held hands again, and then I said, 'Mother, I was horrible to you when I was little. That day when you stood at the door of Dad's house? I said I hated you. And do you know what she said, Robert?"

"What?"

"'Don't worry about it, Jeremy.' Amazing, right? Don't worry about it, Jeremy!"

"That's wonderful," Robert said.

"I felt better right there and then, but there's more. We were sitting there and she ate a meal, slept and woke up. And then I asked her, 'Mother. Why'd you leave? Why didn't I live with you?'

Robert smiled.

"She squeezed my hand and do you know what she said? That she and my father had a bitter divorce, he wouldn't give her all three of us, and they thought it was best to keep the girls together. She said, 'I wanted you, Jeremy. I hated the arrangement. I'm truly sorry.' And then we both cried."

Jeremy and Robert looked at each other for a moment, and Robert said, "That's fantastic, Jeremy."

"Yes!" he said, and then his face became more serious. "You know, I came to treatment to deal with this and now I did. What was that? Three sessions? Four sessions?"

"Right. Have you thought about Emma?" Robert said.

"What does this have to do with her?"

"That's a big thing, no?"

"This was momentous, with my mother. Aren't you happy for me?"

"I am, Jeremy," Robert said, but he knew his face wasn't entirely convincing.

"You're not. Not completely. I know why, too. If I get happy, you lose a client, right?"

"It's not that, Jeremy. I don't keep people for longer than they want to be here."

"So?"

"Listen. I'm really glad you heard what you needed to hear from your mother, but we need to stay on this, that's all. Give it some more time."

"I just want you to be happy for me. Is that too much to ask?"

It wasn't too much to ask, and Jeremy didn't come back to therapy for a month. Robert didn't know if Jeremy would come back at all.

Was I happy for him? Robert asked himself. Yes, I was, but not completely.

Why?

And then he knew: Jeremy's situation played into one of the great mysteries of therapy.

It had to do with ghosts, so to speak, and Robert planned to explain that to Jeremy, if he saw him again.

For now, this is what it was: Jeremy's mother left. That was his issue. Now he'd left treatment. Would that be mine?

It always stung a little when patients prematurely stopped therapy.

At times like these, Robert turned to his writing to mentally change the subject. Often, to a period of history that intrigued him, World War II.

And again, he thought of the park in Berlin and of an old man sitting on a bench, while a group of happy children ran by.

II

Robert had always liked to write.

During a one-year period in his early twenties, he drove a taxi at night in New York City, and he spent the days reading and, at times, writing. He lived in a railroad studio in Soho, three rooms that were four-hundred square feet. The studio had no sunlight but eleven-foot-high ceilings and large windows, and to him it felt like a sublime hideaway. His bedroom looked out on a bucolic courtyard that faced the well-landscaped backyards of the Sullivan Street townhouses on the next block, and there were trees, birds and squirrels.

Robert would wake up late and he had the luxury of a free day until five o'clock, when he had to prepare for his shift. He immersed himself in plays that year, those of Williams and O'Neill most of all. He read *A Streetcar Named Desire* and *Mourning Becomes Electra* again and again. He also read the works of Miller, Albee, Inge, Hellman and the contemporaries, including Shepard and Mamet. His taxi schedule precluded the possibility of having a true social life, and the scale of the apartment limited that as well; it was large enough for a tryst but not quite enough for an easy cohabitation. And aside from a lover he'd see now and then, Robert was quite happy to tuck himself away, alone, and read. The classic American plays, filled with conflict, misery and love, seemed a good substitute for more meaningful and sustained human contact.

During that time, he wrote a few small scenes and one-act plays as well, beginner's attempts. He never showed them to anyone and he understood writing to be nothing more than an engaging hobby. But over time he gained a preliminary understanding of dramatic structure and playwriting.

Decades later, he spotted a memoir in a bookstore. It was called *Defying Hitler* by a man named Sebastian Haffner.

He read it and was so moved by Sebastian's story that he adapted *Defying Hitler* into a play, the first dramatic writing he'd done since his twenties. The work had a staged reading at The New York Theatre Workshop in Manhattan, and the audience of theater professionals reacted favorably.

Who was Sebastian?

He was a noted nonfiction writer in London in the 1940s, but he was born and raised in Germany. He kept a journal during the years of Hitler's rise. His idea was to privately note what was happening around him.

He wrote of unpleasant incidents: being in the library when a man came in and said all the Jews had to leave. Sebastian wasn't Jewish but walking home that day, he wondered why he hadn't said anything. He'd just let it happen. Or another incident in a dance hall, when he and a girlfriend were forced to leave. He thought, Why are we all just standing by and doing nothing?

One event that happened before he left Germany was the day that he and his girlfriend, Charlie, who was Jewish, were sitting on a park bench in Berlin. It was a beautiful day, Sebastian had his arm around her, and they were trying to make Germany disappear. For a few hours, they just wanted to be two lovers in the park.

But then it was ruined. A group of schoolchildren ran by. They saw Sebastian and Charlie on the bench and enthusiastically shouted out *"Juda verrecke!"* (Jews perish!). The children didn't know what Charlie's religion was. Sebastian understood that they had merely shouted out what they thought was a spirited greeting of the times, and then they bounded off. But they broke the spell of the moment.

Soon after, Sebastian left Germany.

After the successful reading of Robert's play, he realized that to take it any further, he needed to obtain the rights to the book. Sebastian had died and Robert wrote to his two children, Oliver and Sarah.

After Oliver had a chance to read the play, he'd contacted Robert and arranged that they speak by phone.

He reached Robert in his office. After their opening salutations, Oliver focused the conversation. "You can have the rights to the book. My sister Sarah was slower to agree, and she has one thing she wants you to change in the play."

"What?"

"There was a scene when Sebastian was with his girlfriend Charlie in the park in Berlin?"

"Yes."

"In your play, you wrote a second scene in the park. In that one, Sebastian, as an old man, returns to the same park and sits on the same bench as he and Charlie once did."

"Yes, I thought that was important."

"You took poetic license with the material; invented a scene that never happened in real life. But that's what writers do, I suppose. It didn't bother me, but she didn't like that. Perhaps you can change it to her satisfaction, or else she wants you to take it out."

There was a momentary pause and then Robert and Oliver made small talk about their lives. Robert thanked Oliver and he said, "That scene in the park. I'll see what I can do."

III

A month later, Jeremy called for an appointment. Robert booked him in and, alone in his office, he sorted out his thoughts.

He decided it all came down to this: Jeremy needed his mother to apologize when he was ten and when she was, say, in her thirties. He finally received the apology recently, when they were both decades older. It wasn't the same.

The strange task for Robert was this: How does the mother in her thirties apologize when she doesn't exist anymore? That was what they needed to figure out. What made it even harder: Robert wouldn't want to solve the mystery by spending hours and having Jeremy try to regress to when he was ten. To do so would cause the alchemy of therapy to lose its magic.

So then, what can I do? Robert wondered.

He knew that Jeremy was lucky to get the apology from his real mother, the one who actually existed, and that in itself could be healing. But in the distorting mirror of human psychology, Robert also knew that the ghost who didn't apologize—the woman in her thirties—was probably more real for Jeremy than the imposter who did. Yes, Robert was actually thinking of the real mother as a kind of imposter!

He wondered, What happens when the ghosts are real, in our minds, and the real people aren't?

□ □ □

Jeremy entered his office the following Friday. As he sat down, he said, "I've been seeing my mother. She's out of the hospital. She's on the mend."

"I'm glad," Robert said.

"I was so angry at you, Robert. I thought you weren't happy for me. Anyway, I wanted to run something by you; a new development."

"All right."

"So. Emma and I have separated. And yes, you and I can discuss her at some point, but that's not why I'm here. I've met a new woman. I wanted to run this by you because, well, you gave me good advice about seeing my mother again and that worked out."

"Tell me about her," Robert said.

"Well, hmm, let's see. What does it mean when you have a feeling something's not going to end well?"

"How so?" Robert said.

"I was sitting at a table in a bar, having a drink. She was standing at the bar. She had black hair pulled back, a long ponytail, red lipstick and a short black dress. I saw her smile at the bartender, all teeth, like a shark. And I had one thought: I want her.

"She turned and smiled at me, and the hair on the back of my neck stood on end," Jeremy continued. "I walked over to her and asked if I could buy her a drink. She said: 'No. I've got to go home. It's my bedtime.' Yeah, right. She took out an eyeliner and wrote her phone number on the palm of my hand." He grinned. "Amazing, right?"

"Yes. Why do you feel it won't end well?" Robert said.

"She just seems like a destroyer, but I'm drawn to her. Do you think I shouldn't do it?"

Robert took a deep breath. "That's the question?"

"Yes."

"I'll answer it, but I need to take a few steps back," Robert said.

"Yes?"

Robert gathered his thoughts and said, "Your mother left you when you were ten and you always needed to understand why. And she finally gave you that answer when you saw her recently?"

"Right."

"You were lucky, Jeremy. Most people never get that kind of closure. But there's still work for us to do. You see, when your mother, in her thirties, didn't explain why she left, well, that was when you became who you are."

"How so?"

"At ten, you perceived her as punishing you when she left, right? And now you're going after a woman who might punish you, the girl in the bar. What's her name?"

"Jen."

"So it's wonderful that your real mother apologized. Truly. But the question is if it changed things."

Jeremy thought for a moment and said, "I don't know what you're talking about. I'm going to see this new woman. That's what I need you to help me with." He smiled. "Do you know what she told me? 'You'd better not be like my last boyfriend. He kissed my sister.'"

Robert's mouth dropped open. "Jen is her name?"

Jeremy nodded and repeated, at the end of the session, "I have a feeling this won't end well."

Alone in his office, Robert asked himself, Is Jeremy dating my patient, Jen? whose boyfriend kissed her sister and drew her in?

That would be impossible. Too much of a coincidence.

But ... if it's true, she'll eat him alive.

And then, oddly, Robert thought: But sometimes people want to be eaten alive.

Robert wondered how to even begin to grapple with that one.

□ □ □

Robert went home and was still thinking about the session, and Jen and Jeremy. He worried about Jeremy, so he changed the subject and thought of his play.

He wanted to resolve any remaining issues right then and there.

Oliver told him that his sister didn't like one of the scenes.

What was it?

Oh yes. Robert put Sebastian back in the park in Berlin as an old man, sitting on the same bench where he'd sat over half a century earlier with his girlfriend, Charlie.

And in the play, some modern-day children came by, and they were shouting.

Sebastian would see them and he'd look away and frown, as old men often do. He was able to hear noise coming out of their mouths but not the words. Their cries were sending him into an old-man world of his own.

And the children who were running by? What were they saying? How did I write it?

Then Robert remembered.

The children were exuberant, and they were running by and shouting, about insects, tag, and ice cream.

THE ROPES

(Robert)

I

When Robert was training at NYU to be a psychotherapist, he interned for seven months at a clinic for people suffering from schizophrenia.

Three mornings a week, he took the subway to the Day Center in Queens. Each of those mornings, upon arrival, he felt his mind go into another world, one that was not altogether unpleasant, but was reminiscent to him of something much darker from his past.

He'd walk through the front door and he'd feel like Alice going down the rabbit hole. Robert would later learn to refer to it as a psychotic transference, as if the delusions of the Day Center clients were in the air, and contagious. Still, there was an exhilarating aspect to arriving each day, a feeling of "see you later!"; saying goodbye to the life he knew and stepping into a parallel universe. He'd smile at the other interns in the hallways and they'd smile back, and sometimes they'd roll their eyes and laugh. They felt it, too.

"Can you describe it?" a fellow student once asked, as Robert sipped coffee with her at an outdoor café in the Village.

"People with schizophrenia have a more intense connection to the physical world than others do," Robert said. "When you're with them, you can't help but feel the same."

"More intense?" she said.

"Yes. And don't you think everyone wants that? Don't you want to be connected to more than your little self? More than to me, me, me?"

"Not that way. I have a cousin with schizophrenia," she said.

Her comment made Robert feel protective of the clients at the Day Center. He gave it one last try. "Take poets ... Isn't that what they do when they write about mountains or streams or love? People want to experience life in such a way as the world itself seems to be talking to them. Well, for the people at the Day Center, it does."

They paid for their coffees, stood, and she began to walk away.

Robert added: "Getting lost in delusions is like losing yourself in another person, like drowning in love and coming out as someone new," but his friend didn't hear him. She was gone.

□ □ □

On the first day of his internship, Robert hadn't known what to expect. He sat with his supervisor, Sharon, in her office. She was an experienced practitioner and seemed rugged and good-natured.

"Have you ever known anyone with schizophrenia? Because you look nervous," she said.

"No, and yes, I am," Robert said.

"Well, now you will. After this, you'll usually be able to tell if someone has this illness from their eyes alone."

Robert looked at her and waited.

"Don't worry," she said. "You'll learn the ropes. Just try to communicate with them. It's easy."

At that moment, one of her colleagues burst into the office. "Sharon. There's a fight in the cafeteria."

"Who?"

"Ernest is strangling Salvador."

Sharon waited a moment and said, "Is it a big strangle or a little strangle?"

The person shrugged and Robert looked at her, wide-eyed.

"All right," Sharon said, and to Robert, "Wait here." She slowly stood and went out.

Ten minutes later she returned.

"It's fine," she said. "Resolved."

"What just happened?" Robert said.

"You looked shocked. The first thing you need to know, Robert: People with schizophrenia are rarely violent. I'll bet that in your time here, you won't see another fight. Violence in this population is a myth. It only happens if they're unmedicated, if they're hallucinating or feeling threatened, which they're not. So, anyway, Salvador sat in Ernest's chair, which pissed him off."

"Big and little strangles? What's that?" Robert said.

"Oh, that! If it were a little strangle, I'd talk to Ernest, and that's exactly what it was, Robert. But if it were a big strangle, say, if Salvador turned blue, then I'd have had to call the authorities and have Ernest committed. That would just be too much."

Weeks later, Robert would tell the story to the other interns and they'd joke with each other, gallows humor: It was a little strangle. Salvador didn't turn blue. We're good.

"Anyway, what were we talking about?" Sharon continued. "Oh yes. Robert, these are wonderful people, most of them. So think of it this way: You have to crack the code. And this is what you'll have to do with those who don't have schizophrenia, when you're in private practice. Figure out what they're about."

"How so?"

"That's a mystery," Sharon said. "Take a person with body dysmorphia. If you tell a person with anorexia, say, 'You look thin,' she'll hear it as 'You look fat.' No one here suffers from anorexia but it's the same principle. Does that make sense?"

"No. That doesn't make sense," Robert said.

Sharon laughed. "All right. Just go talk to them. You'll figure it out."

Robert left her office and, at a payphone, called home to check his answering machine. There was no message from Carolyn. It had been three years since their relationship had ended. Still, falling in or out of love was a process—perhaps another kind of code, he thought—and he couldn't help but check his machine, even if he knew it was of no use. He felt that even a casual greeting from Carolyn would have reassured him. But Carolyn was long over him. You've been on this for way too long, he thought. You're in a loop that keeps repeating. Move on.

He hung up the phone and entered the cafeteria for the first time. There were fifty tables with twenty-five or so people scattered loosely about, and there was a table in front with coffee, cereal, and milk.

Robert spotted an elderly woman sitting alone at a table. She had a faraway gaze. He approached her and sat down.

"How are you?" he said.

"I miss Texas," she said.

"Oh? What do you miss about Texas?" Robert said.

"The snow," she said.

Robert was going to reply but she turned away. He wondered, Is there something to understand here?

No, he thought, I'm not going to ask myself how often it snows in Texas. I know it does, once in a great while, but it's not about that.

Then he thought, Perhaps she's actually saying, I don't want to talk to you, and her comment was a shorthand; a blow-off.

Was that it?

He didn't know, but sitting there, he thought back—for he wanted this awkward conversation to disappear.

He'd met Carolyn five years before, in Mandarin class at Georgetown University, a full year of Chinese in eight hot summer weeks. The class only had nine students and he noted her immediately. She was an American of Greek descent, with striking features: black hair, a long nose and shining brown eyes, but it was her energy that struck him most of all; she was exuberant and fully alive.

He noted that she was aware of Robert as well. He was more adept than she was at languages, he spoke fluent Italian, and he saw her take note of his easy facility with Chinese; how he answered their two teachers' questions—the upbeat, native-Chinese professor, a woman, who taught for the first hour and a half, and the forlorn American professor, a man, who taught for the final hour and a half each day.

The second professor's objective seemed to be to keep them from being overwhelmed by the amount of Chinese they'd had to assimilate from the previous session. One day, he explained how he'd come to get his PhD in the field: he'd obtained a bachelor's degree, then a master's degree, and he found he'd put in so much work up to that point that he'd just continue, and this led to the enormous task of getting his PhD, which he did because, "again, I'd put in so much work that I couldn't stop."

Robert watched Carolyn's reaction to the professor's story, describing his life as a snowball that had rolled down the wrong hill, and Robert imagined that he could feel her judgment, as in: Who lives their life that way? How did he not take the bull by the horns? Why does he look so depressed? Her derisive and slightly amused smile at their professor's plight made her attractive to Robert, even though he related to the man: At that point in Robert's life, he felt stuck, not knowing what he'd do, aside from learning Chinese.

One day Carolyn came to class wearing a white blouse with jeans and brown sandals, and the blouse was open one button too many. He could see her white lace bra and part of her breast. Don't do that, he thought, but she'd seen him looking down her shirt and she smiled. After class, she said, "How do you like it? The class?"

"I do," he said, and they stared at each other.

Robert had the impression that she was attracted to him and he was to her as well, and he'd later realize that his attraction was not only physical but aspirational.

In his life up to that point, he could never shake a feeling of *I'm stuck. I'm paralyzed. I'll never be able to do anything.* He suspected that it had to do with his relationship with his father, but he hadn't put it all together. Carolyn clearly didn't have any such inertia or dread, and that impressed him. She seemed ready to grab onto her life with both hands.

He and Carolyn became study partners and soon, lovers.

The woman who missed Texas because of the snow had her back to him. He thought, I should get up, but then she made a quarter-turn in his direction, they nodded at each other, and he stayed in the chair.

Again, he thought back to that summer when he'd met Carolyn at Georgetown. He thought, There were so many ways I could have fallen in love with her but I didn't. Not at first.

What were they?

Attending class for three hours a day in the ridiculous Washington summer heat, and the sensuality of their wet clothes when they walked together after class. It was a feeling: we're in this together.

Then there was the seductive thrill of a near-impossible task: learning a year of Chinese in two months. This stretched his brain and attention, which translated to his having a hyperawareness of the world around him, and she was in it: her speech, thoughts, gestures, body, movements, and their conversations all made a vivid impression.

There was a small sandwich shop on O and Prospect, and she took him there. On her recommendation, they had turkey melts and cortados and as they ate, she said, wide-eyed, "Can you believe what we're doing?" and she laughed, an explosive burst. He saw the animation in her eyes and he thought, This would make any man fall in love with her.

But he didn't.

Not then.

There was the day they took a break to see the enormous Andy Warhol *Mao*, downtown. Nixon had reopened relations with China a decade before, the Middle Kingdom was stirring everyone's minds and imaginations, and he and

Carolyn were in the vanguard. They gazed up at the immense canvas with wonder and awe and, later, she turned to him outside the new I.M. Pei wing of the National Gallery, the outer wall forming a plane that looked as thin as a sheet of paper, and she said, "I'm going to live and work in China!" She was wide-eyed, exuberant, empowered and sexy, but still, it only went so far.

And there were the long nights they spent in her bed. She rented the recessed level of a house on P Street. She'd light candles and play Keith Jarrett's *Köln Concert*, and the long dank basement felt like a cathedral. The sex was powerful, too, and even more so for the weak air conditioning. He'd watch the sweat bead on her breasts and stomach, and after they'd finish, she'd tell him stories of her childhood, her sister who'd dropped out of school to be an artist, to the consternation of her father—whom she described as Athenian and stubborn. It was, all in all, remarkable; slated to be remembered as an intoxicating summer; a memorable affair.

And then one morning, everything changed.

He'd stayed over the night before, the sun had come up, and he asked if she had a razor he could borrow. She came into the bathroom, partially dressed, and she handed him a razor and a can of shaving cream from the medicine cabinet. Then she leaned against the wall of her tile bathroom and watched him. He put on the shaving cream and began to shave.

Carolyn said, "You're not putting water on your face first?"

"No," Robert said.

"Don't you even know how to shave?"

Years later, when he was long over her, he'd remember that morning and think: God, she was impossible. But in the moment, her words weren't off-putting but registered as a code, one that he didn't understand but had been waiting for. He couldn't explain exactly what it all meant but, suddenly, he was in deeper.

He looked at the woman who missed Texas because of the snow, and he stood and walked out of the cafeteria.

It's over with Carolyn, he told himself again. Stay in the present. Stay with what's real.

□ □ □

A month passed at the Day Center, then another, and Sharon, his supervisor, wished him a happy three-month anniversary at the clinic.

That day a man in his fifties, disheveled and wearing a hoodie, called out to Robert in the hallway. "Hey. Come here," he said, and Robert approached him.

He said, under his breath, "I've been a spy and an astronaut and this I know: if you give an NYU student $14.25 she'll do anything." Then he walked away.

Robert laughed but then his face quickly snapped back. Does he know I'm at NYU? he thought. It was a bit creepy.

Robert tried to analyze the words, as Sharon had suggested. He asked himself: What was the code? And was there even a code at all?

He thought it out. The man saying, "I've been a spy" may signify *I'm an outcast. I watch the world go by and I see things others don't see, but I don't always tell others what I see.*

Robert thought, Check. That was a standard template for those with schizophrenia. They observed everything around them and they kept much of what they saw to themselves.

"I'm an astronaut," as in: *I'm not completely on this planet.* Well, Robert thought, that was pretty much the case.

And "if you give an NYU student $14.25, she'll do anything."

In school the next day, he mentioned it to a classmate, Samantha, who smiled and said, "No, it's not true. You have to give me at least $20.49 for me to do anything," and they laughed. But Robert wondered if that man knew that he and Samantha were doing anything, not for $14.25 or $20.49, but for the price of the master's degree at NYU, tens of thousands of dollars. Was that it? No, the man couldn't have meant that. Or did he mean that we'd do anything to be interns, such as paying to spend a few months at the circus? Observing people like him in their psychologically-flamboyant but troubled lives?

It was impossible to know, but Robert concluded that this:

I've been a spy and an astronaut and this I know: if you give an NYU student $14.25 she'll do anything, was code for this:

I see you. Do you see me?

□ □ □

Robert's father had never taught him how to shave.

That morning in Georgetown, when Carolyn called him out on his shaving technique, he'd stood in her bathroom and felt humiliated and he was flooded with regret.

His father had been a good man but had problems with his son. It was that he preferred women to men, the result, Robert felt, of Robert's grandmother dying of an aneurism when his father was thirty-one, and his father's resultant yearning for the feminine. He became much closer to Robert's sister, and his attitude toward Robert varied from being aloof to disdainful—the latter, often exhibited in his unsolicited career advice. His father, successful in business, expected Robert to follow in his footsteps. Robert expressed a desire to be a therapist, which his father let him know, repeatedly, "wasn't a real thing to do," and the older man's skewed ideas slipped into Robert's value system and took root. This would lead to Robert delaying his pursuit of psychotherapy for years.

Robert knew, on some level, he had so much he needed to resolve regarding that relationship before he'd ever be empowered as a man; before his real life could ever begin. In the meantime, he was destined to experience the legacy of his connection to his father: feeling murky and confused all through his twenties.

When he and Carolyn sat in class that summer, or when they did three hours of homework together, when they sat in a café, looked at the Warhol *Mao* in the National Gallery, or when they had sex, he was at each moment taken by the power and vitality of their connection and it ended there.

But that morning when they were in her bathroom and she commented on his shaving, it registered as a code, but as only a hint, a mere whisper.

At that moment he knew:

This alpha woman will push me—will obnoxiously push me—to deal with things I don't even know I have to deal with. It has to do with my father, somehow. This will hurt and it won't be easy or desirable, but she'll take me where I need to go.

And then, as fast as the thought had appeared, it was gone.

Still, when he left Carolyn's apartment later that morning, her comment, don't you even know how to shave? had morphed into a simple euphemism in his mind: I'm really into her.

And there it was, finally.

He loved her.

II

In the third month of his internship, Robert continued to try to get to know the clients at the Day Center or, as he thought of it, to decipher the codes. In other words, he was still trying to understand people with schizophrenia. The clients were elusive but kind and interesting. He felt he was there to learn and, if possible, to help.

Sharon had asked him to look after Melvin, an enormous and powerful man with severe schizophrenia. He wouldn't be at the Day Center for long. Two months later, he'd try to walk off a three-story roof, not to kill himself but apparently as a sort of informal test of the laws of gravity. Someone saw him and stopped him, and then it would be decided that the world was simply too dangerous for him. Soon after, he was committed to a psychiatric facility.

Robert guessed that Melvin had likely been the victim of severe, early-childhood violence. He was barely able to form sentences. Every day Robert would pick him up from his nearby dormitory and walk him to the Day Center. Robert would offer him a Life Saver on their walks, which Melvin would take. When they arrived at the Day Center, Robert would walk him to the cafeteria, choose a seat for him and prepare a bowl of cereal, which Melvin was unable to do for himself. Once, Robert forgot to give him a spoon and noticed Melvin, five minutes later, still staring at the bowl, waiting, unable to ask. This went on for a few weeks.

One day during their walk from the dormitory to the Day Center, Melvin began to piece words together. He said, "You're a moose."

"I'm a moose, huh?" Robert replied.

And the next day, Melvin said, "You're a moose. I'm a stronger moose."

Sitting with Sharon later that week, Robert casually mentioned those interactions and some other small phrases Melvin had uttered. "It's strange, right?"

"I think it's murderous ideation," Sharon said, as calmly as if she were saying, Beneath the surface of one of Saturn's sixty-two moons, Ganymede, there is an ocean.

"Murderous ideation? Huh?"

"Yes. He's thinking of murder in some form related to you. But don't worry."

Robert took a moment and considered that Melvin was massive, powerful, and psychotic, and was thinking of murder, related to him. Bad combination. Robert marveled as he often did at the constitution of people like Sharon, who chose to work with this population and could take this type of thing in stride—but he couldn't.

He looked at his supervisor and said, "The thing is, Sharon, murder's kind of a trigger word for me." He waited for her to smile but she didn't. "I'm not cool with this. In fact …," he said, taking a deep breath to gather himself before continuing, "I'm not picking up Melvin anymore."

"But he doesn't even have access to a murder weapon," she said.

"How about his hands?"

"Well, if you think so," she said.

"I think so."

Robert also met Jesse, a man for whom inside was out and outside, in. Jesse had no filter and he voiced both his intended thoughts and his inner dialog. One day Robert engaged Jesse about sports and Jesse tried to play along. "I wonder if the Knicks won?" Jesse said, and he quickly followed it with, out loud, "He's staring at me in response to my question about the Knicks. Does that mean they won?"

Robert found this mental flaw, and Jesse himself, endearing and interesting, but their interaction would only be a sketch. The next time Robert saw Jesse and said, "How are you today?" Jesse looked Robert up and down and said, "Ah huh," as if he were a doctor making a disappointing diagnosis, and Jesse never talked to him again.

Robert understood, by then, that this was common with people at the Day Center. The clients didn't sustain connection and would usually cut interns off. Still, Robert tried to determine what had gone wrong. He grappled with his role and was sad to think that there was no way for him not to violate Jesse's psychological space; Jesse surrendered it so freely. Complete transparency was the template through which he interacted with the world. And not only that, Robert thought, but more hauntingly, this: He knows. Robert sensed that Jesse could anticipate him, as he seemed to anticipate everyone who approached. Robert saw that, to Jesse, concern for him was what people do, what interns do, and it was so-called help. But Jesse, aware of the nakedness of his own mind, found all such interactions distasteful.

He has no game. And he knows, Robert thought.

He wondered if all of the clients at the Day Center had the same awareness. Not Melvin, of course, but the others. This question was answered when Sharon suggested that he spend time with Lois, a balding, obese woman.

"I don't want to talk to you," Lois said when Robert sat down beside her. And then she added, "I'm fat, I've never had a job and have never had a relationship. What else do you want to know?"

Robert asked Sharon about Lois later that day. He told her about his interactions with her, and with Jesse.

"She's a hard one," Sharon said affectionately.

"But she knows what's going on," Robert said. "So does Jesse."

"Schizophrenia usually manifests in the early twenties for men and the mid-twenties for women," Sharon said, "so all of our clients have been educated; they're all literate, they read. It just came upon them in their lives. Their delusions come and go, worse for some than others." She smiled gently and added, "Last week, Lois told me that the seagulls were singing her show tunes ... But apart from extreme cases like Melvin, they know that their brains are not quite right and the life that most people take for granted is closed to them. So, yes, Lois knows. Jesse knows."

"Then what can I hope to accomplish with her, or with any of them? What can I do for them?"

"Communicate," she said. "Help them when you can. Be with them. I have a secret plan: to hopefully convince you to work with this population instead of becoming a therapist. But even if you don't, you'll learn things here. You'll grow to love them, too."

"I'll grow to love them?"

"You'll see. Think of it this way. If there's a scale of paranoia from one to one hundred, they live at ninety-seven or ninety-eight on the scale, and you and I are maybe at seven or eight, maybe fifteen, but it's one scale. It's the same scale. You're not that different from them. We're not."

"OK. Thank you," Robert said, and as he left her office he thought, She has no idea of the psychological path I took to get here. It would make her head spin.

III

Robert moved to New York after DC, and he and Carolyn kept in touch. A year later she moved to Taiwan, taking a job with Ernst and Young. She invited him to come to see her, specifically, for a month. He was astounded that at twenty-seven she'd had the wherewithal to find employment and take up residence in Asia. He wasn't doing much at the time and was up for anything, so off he went.

She lived with an elderly Chinese woman who believed Robert had come from a past life to see her. That was odd yet reassuring. Carolyn liked her living arrangement: the old woman was kind and helped her to improve her Chinese. Carolyn found Robert an apartment, which would ensure their privacy, and steered him to an ESL school, where he was hired to teach English.

They had several intimate weeks together, the strangeness of Taipei adding to the feeling of being lost in a dream. Nights, by the streetlights where he lived, hundreds of bats would dive just above their heads, and there were the sights and smells, the unimagined food scents wafting off the local markets, so odd as to be disorienting—and Robert realized that olfactory jolts were more unsettling than other sensory stimuli. They also experienced the strange, local culture, such as how, in the restaurants, the waiters would speak to them so loudly, as if screaming, as compared to the volumes at which waiters tended to speak back home in English—and this was in marked relief to their softer tones with each other during their dinners. And then there was this: customers spit on the floor in the restaurants in Taipei; again, exotic and off-putting. They were alone in a strange world.

Then there were the long nights in his room. Once, she stood up and danced for him to Chinese rock and roll on the radio. He thought, This is a moment in time, and we're free here.

Another time she randomly said, on the tatami that served as his bed, "Don't you know you that in life, you can do whatever you like?" and he thought, She senses the situation. But no, I don't.

On an evening in the third week, walking to a local restaurant for dinner, she stopped, pointed to a nearby storefront and said, "It's a hair salon. The men sit in the chairs and grope the hairdressers, and they tip them for that. Or for more; I think they might have sex with them, too, and for that they pay extra." She met his gaze. "Do you know, Robert, Japanese men come to Taiwan to do that? After everything that went down between the Chinese and the Japanese in World War II." She stopped, speechless at the thought. Then she turned to him and said, "Do you know what I think of Japanese men who come here to touch, let alone sleep with, these Chinese women?"

"What?" he said.

"I want to slap them. No, you know what I want to do? I want to throw up *on* them."

Robert laughed. He found Carolyn to be over the top, but what amused him most was that she'd stressed not the act but the trajectory. Where? *On* them. He supported her passion, loved her for it, in fact, and that love allowed him to focus mostly on the exuberance in the anger.

Just then they passed a pit bull leashed to a storefront, and it barked and lunged at Carolyn. Robert moved her to the outside and put himself between her and the animal. He would have done anything to protect her. Was that what love was? he wondered, but he knew that this was just a moment in time. Their relationship had to end, it couldn't last, not because she was crazy and wanted to throw up on Japanese men, but because he wasn't her equal. He knew, over time, this would make her an actual obstacle in his path. He sensed it there, on the Taipei streets. It was as if he were trying to grasp a theorem: Does like become like? More specifically, if you're in love with a person who has the qualities you'd want for yourself, power, strength, and independence, does loving her confer those qualities upon you? He intuitively knew the answer, so the theorem was really a tombstone. He thought, I'm suspended here in Taipei with this woman, and it will end soon. This lent a poignancy to their time together, because he didn't want to lose her and he knew he would.

"Dogs never like me," she said, as they took their seats in the restaurant. "Why do you think that is?"

"Maybe they pick up your anger," Robert said.

"I don't think so. It's not that."

"Well then, maybe they go by scent," he said.

"Are you saying I don't smell lovely?"

"No. You do," he said, and they laughed.

Yes, he thought, the way she looked at him, the way she laughed, the way she moved, it was a moment, suspended. But, he thought, Tick tock. He couldn't endure being the weaker man with the stronger woman for long, and he suspected she wouldn't have him be that, either.

On their way home after the meal, she skipped in the street. He looked around, in awe of the incredible Chinese landscape she'd opened up to both of them and he thought, The world is hers for the taking.

Right on schedule, three and a half weeks after his arrival, they were on his tatami after sex and Carolyn said, "I invited you to come here for a month to visit me. I have my life here. You're leaving next week, right?"

Robert thought for a moment and said, "I'm in the middle of teaching a course."

"So? Your visa is for one month," she said.

Robert visualized going back to the US and dreaming of Carolyn for the rest of his life. He thought, That won't do. He knew that his resistance to her original schedule would cause the relationship, and him, to crash and burn, but he felt that such an outcome was still preferable to going home and loving her, unrequited, forever. So, no, he decided he wouldn't go. He said to Carolyn, "I'm not leaving. I'm breaking the deal."

"You're not," she replied, and she proceeded to take nail polish out of her handbag and paint her toenails red. He found that remarkable. It felt to him as if she were indicating, this is all about me; you're barely here.

He wondered if she was truly that nonchalant and cold-hearted, but a few days later, he knew, for she reported him to the authorities for violating the terms of his one-month visa.

He was called down to an office and interviewed by a middle-aged government official who spoke to him in Chinese.

"Why did she report you?" the man said.

Robert shrugged.

"You care for her?" the man said.

"*Dui.*"

"And you're employed as a teacher?"

Robert nodded and the man studied him. Robert thought, This is good; unlike in America, teachers actually count for something in Chinese culture.

There was an awkward moment and the man looked deep in thought. And then, completely out of left field, he said, "I once loved a woman when I was young. She just invited me to her wedding with someone else."

They exchanged a smile.

Robert wondered if he'd attend Carolyn's wedding with someone else. Perhaps he would. Or maybe—who on earth does she think she is, marrying someone else?—he wouldn't. His mind was veering into the realm of disorganized, racing thoughts. It felt dangerous.

He turned to the man. "Will you attend?"

The official shrugged. "I don't know," he said, and they smiled at each other. It occurred to Robert: I don't want to be carrying all of this twenty years later, as he's still doing. I'm right not to leave.

"You can remain in Taipei," the man finally said. "Stay away from her, though," he added, and he stamped Robert's passport.

Robert lived in Taiwan for six more months.

He dropped out of Carolyn's life and of everyone she knew. He became dangerously isolated, working as a teacher by day, which included transcribing Beatles lyrics, playing the songs, and having his students sing along for syntax and grammar, while steering them away from the Beatles poetically-licensed "ain'ts" and inappropriate "don'ts." And nights, crying, mostly, beneath the bats that ducked and weaved above the streetlights.

He found a large volume of Nietzsche in the English language bookstore and he'd read it every night in his room. He loved the way Nietzsche turned a phrase and defied logic, such as "People should hope to have one weakness: the weakness of their fear," or the classic, "What doesn't kill you makes you stronger." He found the writings mesmerizing and invigorating.

He'd later hear somewhere that Nietzsche had ended up, later in life, trying to get naked in front of a rain puddle to take a swim. He'd realize that this was not the best role model.

In that era, China had opened up for tourism for the first time since its revolution thirty-five years before. Westerners could finally travel to China, but only in large tour groups. But through the Taipei grapevine, Robert learned of a loophole. He could obtain a visa in Hong Kong to travel through China alone. It was originally intended for the ethnically Chinese, residents of Hong Kong who were visiting their relatives, but stray non-Chinese and Westerners were able to avail themselves of it as well. The only catch was that the visa would be on a separate slip of paper in the passport, and he'd have to throw it away after the trip. Taiwan, the Republic of China, didn't allow travel to the People's Republic of China at the time, and if Taiwanese officials learned that he'd gone there, they wouldn't let him back in.

He and Carolyn had discussed going to China together, but that was clearly not going to happen. From the summer class in Georgetown and another year of Chinese classes there, he'd learned to say such things in Mandarin as "the Chinese economic system is agrarian" and then, in Taiwan, he'd filled in the gaps in his vocabulary and fluency. His Chinese was good enough at that point and he decided he'd go to China alone.

There, he'd meet people on the streets and in the restaurants of Beijing. He'd have discussions with them in Chinese, and he would unravel.

IV

Months into his internship at the Day Center, Robert met the most high-functioning client there, Albert. He was the only clinic member who was able to sustain a relationship, he had a girlfriend, and the only one who held down a job, part-time.

One day he told Robert his story.

"At twenty-four, I had a job in an ad agency," Albert said. "I began to feel, on the street, that a force of some kind was after me. It seemed to be a quirk at first, and I'd mention it to my coworkers in a hidden form, so as not to arouse their suspicions. I'd say, 'Do you ever feel like someone's following you?' But then one day, I heard a terrifying voice behind me telling me that it was going to kill me. I was too scared to turn around and look at it, so I ran home and that was the end. My life fell apart. I never returned to my job.

"My girlfriend Loretta and I met in the store where I work now. I'm a cashier. She's from a difficult background as well."

"Difficult?" Robert said.

"From violence," he said, and he didn't elaborate.

Another time Albert said, "Do you know, Robert, I don't need to listen to music because I can replay entire songs in my head? I can specifically recreate, say, the Stevie Wonder tune 'I Was Made to Love Her,' and I can choose to either listen to the whole song or I can hear separate tracks in my mind: just the drums, the bass, or the vocals."

Robert wondered if this were possible and thought how Albert conformed to a stereotype he'd often heard about people with schizophrenia: that they're all highly intelligent. Robert had learned at the clinic that people seemed to fall into the same range of intelligence, some more, some less, as those who weren't afflicted with the illness.

During that period, one of Robert's professors had talked to his class about self-care. He'd said that interns and therapists needed to get enough sleep for their own stability, and so as not to have bags under their eyes. "You mustn't appear to be unhealthy. It can worry people." It was winter then and the Day Center was a stressful environment. Robert wasn't taking good care of himself or getting sufficient sleep, so he purchased a tinted moisturizer that he applied to his face. No one noticed, neither friends nor family, and he felt it gave him a subtle glow of color.

One day he ran into Albert in the hall, who said, "It's quite remarkable, Robert. Your facial tone is half a shade darker than the backs of your hands."

Robert stared at him for a moment and then, flabbergasted, walked away. But if he had any doubt before, he didn't any longer. He thought, Albert can definitely separate the tracks of the Stevie Wonder song in his head.

V

Robert left Taipei and made his way to Beijing.

What he found extraordinary there was the paranoia in the air and, in that way, it was very different from Taiwan or America. It started from the moment he set foot in Beijing. As he stepped off the train from Canton, three men with cameras surrounded him on the platform, aggressively photographing him as they moved around him in a circle, like paparazzi. At the time, it was obvious that they were from the government; China was a third-world country, everyone was poor, wore blue Mao suits that were jeans jumpsuits, and no one had technology or cameras. He watched them circling him like vultures and he thought, OK, I'm here as an individual, not in a group, and the government wants me to know they have an eye on me. Fine, he thought, I have nothing to hide. But from that moment, his time in Beijing took on a more sinister cast in his mind.

There was the teenage boy Robert met one day on the street who enthusiastically offered to show him around Beijing. Robert recognized the boy as displaying the custom of *ying gai*, noblesse oblige. Back in Taipei, two college students, interested in America, had once offered him a similar tour of Taipei when he met them jogging on the track of Tai Da, the university. Robert learned that it was a compulsory remnant of Confucianism: helping a guest. But in Beijing it was different. The boy said, in Chinese, "I can't come to your hotel, I'm not permitted. You can't come to my work. So tomorrow meet me here, by this tree."

Sensing the boy's fear, Robert tried to talk him out of it, not wanting to get him into trouble, but the boy insisted. Luckily—from Robert's point of view—the boy didn't show up the next day.

There was the brave couple in a restaurant who sat next to Robert at a common table and spoke to him while covering their mouths with their hands, as if whispering. They asked him where he was from and what America was like, and were clearly happy to talk to a foreigner. But Robert could see that the conversation aroused suspicion from those around them, all of whom were Chinese. He saw fear flash across the couple's faces, and he had a sense that the conversation could somehow compromise them.

There were the soldiers Robert saw in Tiananmen Square, one of whom leaned over and literally wretched at the sight of him. This was not too long after the Cultural Revolution, and *yángguǐzi*, "foreign devil," was still in the everyday Chinese vernacular. They'd been taught for years that non-Chinese were the enemy, apparently unaware that tourism was gearing up.

The only person who wasn't completely apprehensive of contact during his entire trip was a woman in her early twenties. She approached Robert as he happened to be walking by a movie theater one day. "Have you seen this movie?" she said in stilted English. "No," he said, and she invited him to see it and bought two tickets. They proceeded to sit through a three-hour propaganda film in Chinese, which felt, to Robert, like ten hours. It was about how horrific colonial China had been before their 1949 revolution. It included Chinese people being beaten and others addicted to "English opium."

After the film, Robert and the woman walked outside, shook hands, and she walked away. Robert sensed, from her completely fearless attitude and from the nature of the film,

that she'd been instructed to take him there by the authorities, a sort of friendly attempt at a cultural education, or
reeducation. He found that strange.

But there was one incident in Beijing that threw Robert
over the line. On the face of it, it was a trivial encounter he
had on a bus. He was holding onto the pole and a refined,
older man grabbed onto the same pole and engaged him
in conversation in Chinese. They spoke about America's
opening to China, and how China would likely change. After
five minutes, a burly teenager boarded the bus, saw them,
took hold of the same pole and aggressively wedged himself
between the two men. The boy's obvious intention was to
separate them, and also to discover what this man might
have been saying to a foreigner. The older man looked
at Robert with a tolerant, weary smile, and limited his
conversation, at that point, to the sights Robert should see
in Beijing.

When Robert got off the bus, he realized that in
a theoretical dispute with authorities, the younger man's
word would carry more weight than the educated man's,
for the latter was speaking to a person who wasn't ethnically Chinese. It was the first time Robert, who was white,
had experienced racism directed at himself. But much
more disturbingly, it was the first time he'd experienced a
totalitarian regime in a personal way, through watching the
older man obviously having to limit what he was free to talk
about on the bus. It roused in Robert a deep sense of terror
and revulsion.

Up until that point in Robert's life, in the West, he under-stood paranoia to be a personal phenomenon. It was the result of one's own, private issues; one's own problem, you might say. For example, if one were neurotic or mentally ill or, say, high.

In China, Robert understood that fear and paranoia were different: ubiquitous and part of the social fabric. Certainly so, in relation to him: the country had been closed to foreigners since its revolution so Robert, white, was experienced as *other* to everyone. And then, of course, China was communist, so a citizen could easily get arrested for expressing unorthodox beliefs. That was baked into every-one's awareness.

And just as the citizens of communist countries censored their thoughts, Robert, the conscientious tourist, eventually found himself observing the local custom. After the incident on the bus, the final straw, he lost his words by a kind of political contagion. He'd taken a much different route to the quotidian fear he'd seen in the average citizen of the People's Republic of China, but the end result was the same.

He formed a mental template for the rest of his time in Beijing.

- I don't want to talk to the people who, like the young thug on the bus, are tools. They don't want to talk to me, anyway.
- I don't want to talk to those who *do* want to talk to me—the teen who wanted to show me around, the couple I spoke to

in the restaurant, or the man on the bus—because I don't want to endanger them, which talking to me could do.
· Therefore, I'll talk to no one.

From that moment on, he'd gaze at people in the streets and in the restaurants of Beijing through veiled, paranoid eyes, with an interiority and apprehension that he'd see, years later, in the clients at the Day Center. His thoughts would run around and around in his head, anger and curiosity born of intense loneliness, for the rest of his trip, but he'd keep those thoughts to himself.

After China, Robert went back to Taipei, packed up his belongings and went home to New York.

There, his paranoia, which he'd experienced as a shared reality in China, flipped back. It was just personal once again. He knew he was out of sorts, but now he felt that he'd merely been turned inside out from a private event: the heartbreak of losing Carolyn.

Still, he experienced New York and America in astonishing relief to Beijing, and this stunned him. Just as Carolyn had awakened in him the stifling nature of his relationship to his father—he noted, after having traveled, that countries themselves had similar issues, and, in effect, that America grappled with its own, with its so-called father issues, quite well. It was suddenly clear to him: while America fell back on caricatured male archetypes, such as those he saw on the movie posters when he got back, for James Bond and Rambo, those tended to have minimal cultural effect. And in this, in America's lack of more authoritarian voices, Robert could see where America was at its most impressive: in Americans' inherent understanding that the dream of the father archetype, too closely applied, would choke them. Even if it's natural to yearn for a guide, a strong hand, a daddy, or a voice to tell you what to do, he knew that there could be no other outcome of such a desire, if fully realized, than debilitating fear and oppression. He'd lived through it on a personal level when he'd put his dreams of being a therapist aside for many years because of his father's bullying and intimidation, and he'd lived through it in his mind and body in Beijing; he'd seen it in the Chinese faces in the restaurants, in the streets, and that day on the bus. He knew, in the deepest way, that a bullying father, or a government acting as one, didn't end well.

He felt he needed to write about this. He needed to get it all down on paper. He thought, If I can write it out, about China, about America, it might win Carolyn back, too. So he knew what he had to do. The problem with the plan was that his thoughts carried too much traumatic import to be readily conveyed.

He'd drink double espressos at midnight at Caffe Dante for inspiration, which was not a very good regime for a balanced and well-regulated body clock. He'd try to write but he'd make mistakes and, writing on a typewriter, he'd have to put in a new sheet of paper and start all over again. Then he'd write a hundred words or so on a fresh page, but would soon have to start from scratch yet again—with more crumpled paper all over the floor.

He wasn't quite sure if his ideas were cogent. He'd seen the film *The Shining*, and knew he wasn't at the Jack Nicholson stage of writing a thousand pages consisting only of the phrase "All work and no play makes Jack a dull boy," but he was aware that he couldn't get things down in the right way.

At two in the morning, he'd often go to the Pyramid Club in the East Village and dance alone. He wasn't talking to anyone in those days. Later, he'd walk home from the Pyramid, from Avenue A, looking behind him, and he often imagined he was being followed. He knew he was paranoid but he'd ask himself, Why did those three men take my picture on the train platform in Beijing?

By then, he'd cut off his family. The last time they spoke, his father had lectured him about his life—"You need to get started"—and Robert had said, "Dad, people on the streets of Beijing are scared to even tell you the time of day," to which his father had suggested that Robert seek therapy. His mother, in their last conversation, had said, "Robert, I'm worried about you," in a quiet voice, but Robert felt that she didn't understand that he was on a mission. And as for his sister, he'd ranted to her on the phone and she'd just cried. So he isolated himself, much as he'd done in Taipei.

And then it all fell apart. He'd simply endured too much trauma and he'd pushed his mind past its breaking point. So Robert checked himself in, and spent six days inpatient, in a psychiatric institution.

His parents came to visit on the second day. They sat with him in his room and no one said much. He could feel how worried they were about him and how much they cared, and he gratefully took it in.

Then his mother mentioned that she'd gone by his apartment and found a Jackson Pollack postcard that had been slipped under his door. She handed it to him and Robert read the card: "Get well, Robert, from your friends at the Pyramid."

He knew he had no friends at the Pyramid, he'd never spoken to anyone there, no one but his family knew he was in the institution, and the postcard had arrived less than twelve hours later.

He wondered where the postcard had come from? Was he really being followed when he thought he was? Did it have to do with the Taiwan/China situation, and his disposable visa? Or was it the manuscript he'd copyrighted that spoke to how Taiwan, "free China," wasn't as free as the Reagan administration would have had people believe at the time? ... Taiwan wasn't as culturally free: several of Robert's female students who had married the *dà érzis*, the oldest sons, complained of their roles as unofficial domestic servants for their live-in in-laws, nor did Taiwan seem to be politically free: Robert learned that the Republic of China didn't have open elections when he lived there. He wondered if that was what the postcard was about?

After his parents left, he stared at it. He found the "Get well, Robert, from your friends at the Pyramid" ominous, but he also found it to be reassuring in an odd way. It made him feel that his distress wasn't merely an isolated situation but had flipped back. He wasn't just a lost individual but there was something larger going on. His mind wandered. He asked himself, is the government concerned with me? and, if one is a bad writer and the government reads what you write because they want to censor you, do you feel like you have a fan? But then he stashed the postcard away; he needed to put the outside world aside and focus on grounding himself, feeling safe, and bringing himself back.

Evenings, he'd go into the dayroom and sit on a sofa in the faint light. There was a record player and a large stack of albums. He'd listen to Richard Pryor live in concert and laugh out loud.

One day he was in his room, on his bed, and a girl in her twenties stuck her head in his doorway and said, "I get the joke now," and she disappeared.

He wondered what she was talking about. He was tempted to just dismiss her as being out of her mind but then he thought, I totally get the joke. To him, it had something to do with the games people play. Just as, when Robert felt his mind breaking down and he'd gone to the institution on 12th Street in the Village, the admitting psychiatrist had asked him what was wrong. He'd said, "I'm depressed," and he'd observed how the doctor seemed so pleased to observe Robert's crisp self-diagnosis. But Robert hadn't been depressed. It was a euphemism for "I don't want to answer these questions. I want to be left alone." And just then, Robert understood something essential about psychology, *everything is moving all the time; nothing is fixed.*

Was he depressed? No. He felt more anxious, if anything, but what did the doctor expect him to say?

"What seems to be wrong, Robert?"

Should he have given him the long version?

"Well, you see, doctor, one day this lovely and sexy woman was standing against the tile wall of her bathroom in a basement in Georgetown. She had no shirt on and she had her arms crossed. I put shaving cream on my face, and she was watching ..."

VI

During his internship at the Day Center, the person Robert was most fond of was a client named Jackson. Jackson had spent most of his life in psychiatric hospitals, the penalty, Robert felt, for trying to kill himself while being nine years old and Black. He was in his fifties.

Jackson suffered from severe schizophrenia and was always on the verge of being banned from the Day Center. He wore a fraying seersucker suit and he chivalrously held women's chairs as they sat down, but he'd also threaten them with violence if they didn't thank him to the level of his satisfaction. This led the director to warn him that if he didn't change his behavior he'd have to leave.

Sharon told Robert to try to get to know him. Robert questioned her about the way he harassed women.

Sharon shrugged and said, "He was probably subjected to unspeakable levels of violence and sexual abuse as a child in those institutions."

"What's going to happen to him?" Robert said.

"What will happen? He'll probably threaten one of the women one time too many, and he'll be kicked out."

"What then?" Robert said.

"In that case, he'd end up homeless and unmedicated. Anyway, try to spend some time with him."

That day Robert nodded to Jackson and he nodded back, and they had a short conversation. Jackson asked Robert what he was doing there. Robert explained that he was an intern and Jackson smiled and burst out laughing. Then, after a moment, Jackson's face changed and he eyed Robert suspiciously. Robert guessed that he was trying to determine if Robert was CIA or from an alien planet sent to spy on him.

After that, their connection mostly consisted of waving to each other and smiling. When Jackson received another warning for harassing female residents, Robert confronted him. "They said you threatened to hit Pamela. You know, if you keep doing that, they're going to throw you out."

"I didn't threaten to hit Pamela," he said, and Robert sensed that Jackson believed his own story.

He was a chain smoker and he'd frequently go outside to smoke. Robert would often follow him there, and one day Jackson let on that he was an expert in ping-pong. He said it again to Robert a week later. "I'm the best ping-pong player in the world." Robert asked Sharon in her office, "Do you think he can really play?"

"Could be. In those snake pits where he spent his life, they probably had ping-pong tables."

Jackson kept bragging to Robert—who did the research and one day, finally said to him, "Do you want to show me how good you are?"

"Yes," Jackson said.

"I know where we can go to play," Robert said. Jackson broke out laughing, and they headed out.

Robert and Jackson took the subway. Sitting together as they traveled across Queens, Robert said, "Why did you try to kill yourself when you were nine?"

"My parents used to beat me very badly," he said, and he shook his head and said quietly, "Very badly."

They reached their stop, got off, and Robert led him to their destination, a ping-pong hall. They rented rackets and a table, and they proceeded to play. They were laughing, shouting, and diving for the balls. Jackson was much better than Robert, often slamming shots over the net, and he soundly beat Robert in four games. He wanted to play more, but Robert had had enough. Jackson insisted and Robert said, "Maybe the owner will play with you. Do you want me to ask him?"

"Yes."

Robert approached the owner and asked him to play with Jackson, and the owner agreed. He and Jackson proceeded to play two games and as they did, Robert noticed a plaque on the wall. He walked over to it and learned that the man was a former Olympian.

When they were finally in the subway on their way back to the Day Center, Jackson said, "I beat him."

"No, you beat me, four times. He beat you in two games," Robert said. "Do you know the owner was in the Olympics? He played ping-pong in the Olympics, and you scored points against him. That's amazing, but he won."

"No. I did," Jackson said.

In that moment, Robert understood that the distance from Jackson feeling he won to, I tried but I lost or, I can do better next time, was a bigger leap than Jackson was able to make; it was the abyss separating him from the world of expansion and possibility. But due to a fluke of biology and a history of physical abuse, it would be impossible for Jackson to ever make that leap. For the rest of the week, he stayed away from Robert, and he let it be known that he was Jesus Christ.

Robert approached him outside one day. Jackson was reading an apocalyptic science fiction book, which he rested on a blue US mailbox as a bookstand. He saw Robert coming and briskly walked away.

Standing there, it struck Robert that when he'd lived in Taipei, a narrative had run through his own mind, not once but many times, but it had always disappeared. Robert's narrative had been more hopeful and less delusional than Jackson's, but it had been as dangerous.

It went like this:

Carolyn likes me but she doesn't love me. If I stay in Taipei it will blow up in my face, but isn't that preferable to leaving and dreaming of her forever?

So don't go back to the States. Stay in Taiwan.

She'll end it and you'll be destroyed. But there's something inside you that needs to be destroyed.

You'll get through it.

And he thought, I'll get through it? It occurred to him what a luxury that was and how lucky he was. Jackson and the others couldn't get through it. They were biologically jinxed.

It was a lesson that hadn't quite occurred to Robert before: some people don't get better.

VII

On the last day of his internship, Sharon and Robert sat in her office. She asked Robert what he thought of his time at the Day Center.

"It was the Magical Mystery Tour," Robert said.

"Do you think you're up to working with this population on a regular basis?"

"No. I find it too upsetting," Robert said.

"How so?"

"Like a whirlwind."

"I see. Then you still intend to be a psychotherapist?" Sharon said.

"Yes."

"Well, then, this experience will help you," she said.

He looked at her.

"You know, the people here tell themselves stories: simple, paranoid stories," she said. "But people in the outside world aren't that different. Every patient you'll ever see tells themselves stories about themselves. You do. You're always thinking about a girl, right? You mentioned her in our first meeting."

Robert was stunned, but then he recalled telling Sharon about Carolyn at his entry interview, which had been more of a psychological-intake interview.

"It's really been over with her for years," Robert said, and he noted that in the past month at the Day Center, he'd been checking much less frequently for her messages on his answering machine.

"Do you remember you told me to find the codes, Sharon?" Robert said. "That's what you said to me on my first day. But there are no codes here that I can see. Take Jackson. He was himself and then he was Jesus Christ. Lois hears seagulls singing her show tunes, but she hates herself and hates everyone. Melvin wants to walk off the roof. They don't have a chance."

"They make progress, but not the same kind of progress that would be open to you or me," Sharon said. "But if that's how you feel, Robert, then you're right not to work with them. But as for the codes—"

"Yes?" Robert said.

"It's your last day. Do you want to tell me more about the girl?"

Robert was taken aback, but he recalled that Sharon had previously been a therapist. He thought for a moment and he said, "This is confidential?"

"Yes," she said, and he proceeded to tell her the story about Carolyn and China. Sharon listened patiently and he spoke for twenty minutes.

When he finally finished, she said, "You've been through a lot. So let me ask you: What were the codes in that story?"

"What do you mean?"

"I mean, we all tell ourselves things in shorthand. As Jackson does," she said.

"Well, I don't think I'm Jesus Christ," Robert said.

"No, but that has meaning in Jackson's mind. So, the codes?"

Robert shrugged.

"Think of your future patients," Sharon continued. "Take a victim of incest who says, 'I prefer to be home alone nights rather than to socialize.' But what she really means, beyond her awareness, is 'I prefer to remain loyal to the person who did this to me, whom I hate, and I'm most loyal when I'm home alone,' where she punishes herself, say, binges. But she doesn't connect all of those dots. I prefer to be home alone nights is a kind of code. That's what I mean. So, what are the dots you can connect in your story? What was it really about?"

"All right," Robert said, and he leaned back in his chair. "Well, I was a weaker person than Carolyn, but I became stronger through losing her, ironically. I always thought she was stronger, but now I'm as strong as she was."

"How did that happen?"

"Through loss—and I landed on a therapist who knew how to focus on what mattered."

"Good. What else?"

"I had father stuff."

"And you're working on it?" she said.

"Carolyn awakened in me the need to and since then, in therapy ... I'm not as angry with my father as I used to be."

"Good. What else?"

"Isn't that enough?" Robert said.

"No," she said.

Robert smiled and rolled his eyes. Then he said, "OK. I was in love with a woman who didn't want me. That shattered me."

"So the story was also about getting your heart broken and coming back from that?" Sharon said.

"Yes."

"Here's the thing, Robert. One day you may—no, one day you will—decide that it was about something else entirely."

"Such as?" he said.

"A story you haven't thought of yet. One day, the story you just told me will be different. You'll reshape it to fit a new situation in your life and it will become a new narrative. And that's what your future patients will be doing in your office."

"They'll be doing what?" Robert said.

"Trying to make sense of something that's changing all the time."

"You know, I once had a feeling for that," Robert said.

"What do you mean?" Sharon said.

"When I crashed and burned, when I was at my lowest point, I viscerally understood: in psychology, the light's always shifting and things are always moving."

"That's good," she said, "so perhaps your past difficulties will give you a head start. In your job as a therapist, Robert, you'll help your patients make sense of things in the same way as you did."

She paused for a moment and then she added, "As for those here, Jesse, Lois, Jackson, they all do it too, they reshape their stories all the time, but," she smiled affectionately, "they do it in collapsed time. So they can only take things so far ..."

"I get it," Robert said.

"Do you?"

"Yes," Robert said. "You're saying that we all make it up as we go, but the clients here, they're just not as good at, well, pulling off their latest fictions."

"Right. Anyway, Robert, I'm talking too much."

"No," Robert said, and he knew it was time for him to go. He stood and said, "I'm grateful to you for everything, Sharon. Thank you," and they shook hands and then they hugged goodbye.

Robert walked to the door, stopped, and said, "May I ask you something?"

"Yes?"

"Do you think we help them here?"

"In our way," she said.

"But people with schizophrenia, they don't get better?" he said.

"No, not quite."

"So?"

"They stay on their meds," Sharon said.

"Yes."

"And people need not to be alone. There's that."

Robert went outside and saw Lois coming up the street. He waited. She was walking with difficulty because of her girth. She eventually reached where he was standing and she stopped and looked up at Robert. Then she rolled her eyes and said, "What do *you* want?" with a level of repulsion that almost made him laugh.

"Nothing. We're good, Lois," he said softly, and she began walking again.

Robert watched her enter the Day Center, and then he turned and headed home.

RECOVERY

The Forgiving

Reconstructions

As a therapist, I see trauma show up often in my patients, in terms of sexual abuse, and breakups and loss.

I've found the psychological injuries that people endure to be unfathomable. But so is the courage with which they often bring themselves back from the abyss.

The first story in this section involves the trauma of sexual abuse, which may be hard for some to read. One of my favorite quotes is from the film *Down by Law*: "It's a sad and beautiful world." Well ... I think sexual abuse is the sad part.

The second story is about the loss of a relationship.

THE FORGIVING

(Catherine, James)

I

Catherine and James hoped to be together for the rest of their lives, but when that became more difficult for them to imagine, they were referred to Robert. They were a handsome couple, and Robert guessed, in their mid-thirties.

"She wanted to come alone," James said by way of introduction, as he sat down in the chair.

"I did," Catherine said, taking a seat on the sofa, "but he asked to join for the first session."

"Let me ask you a question," James began. "If we come to couple's therapy, will it help us stay together or will it break us up?"

"It can be either," Robert said.

"Because I'm not doing this if it will end the relationship. We don't want to break up," James said, and Catherine nodded in agreement.

"Couple's therapy gets at the truth of what's going on. Do couples ever break up? Yes, but if the relationship were to end, it would end more gracefully. With less acrimony," Robert said.

"That's not good enough. Let's go," James said, and he stood.

"No," Catherine said. "I'm staying."

She met James's eyes and shook her head, and James left.

"Well, now it's just me," Catherine said. "But if I want to bring James back for couples therapy, will that be possible?"

"Yes," Robert said.

"Good," Catherine said. "So, I'll start. I'm here to figure out if I can forgive James. If I can't, I'll have to leave him."

She paused and said, "It's awkward to come in and talk to a stranger, a man, about sex."

Robert waited and Catherine launched into her story.

"James and I have been together for two and a half years and, um, we were bored in bed," she began. "Then James had this idea: swinging. Sex with strangers. But you know, men are weird enough to me on the street, so I didn't think I'd want to have a one-off at a party. But he kept after me and I finally agreed.

"He made the arrangements for this event in Chelsea and on a Friday night, we went to this apartment," she said. "There were all these people ... You know, they weren't completely repulsive to me ... There were mattresses on the floors in the different rooms—but after a few minutes, I said

'James, I don't want to do this,' and he said, 'We talked about it, blah, blah, blah.' He went to get us drinks. I stood there in the corner, like a nun, and this guy was looking at me. It was almost as if he could read my mind. Maybe he thought I was a challenge in some sick way? Anyway, James came back, gave me the drink and then he was off! I went to look for him and found him in the next room, making out with a girl. Motherfucker. So I drifted back and sat down. There was something in the drink. Things got a little foggy."

"You were drugged?" Robert said.

"Yes, definitely ... But I sat there and thought I needed to loosen up. That guy came over, the one who was looking at me, and he started talking to me. And, well, to make a long story short, I fucked him." She shook her head. "It was pretty bad but it didn't last long.

"James found me," she continued. "He'd done the same with that girl, and I remember I was smiling and laughing as we left. But now something has shifted in me. I agreed to go to the party, so it's on me, right? I'm not saying it's totally his fault, but I resent him."

Catherine excused herself to go to the bathroom. When she came back, she looked out the window. Robert's office was on the second floor and there was an antique shop across the street. "Look at that," she said, and Robert joined her. In the store window was a gray granite Buddha, just short of three feet tall. "Quite forbidding, that Buddha," she said, and Robert agreed. They sat back down.

"I love James, so what do I do now?" she said.

"We need to figure out what buttons were pushed at the party, beyond the obvious. Do you have any sexual trauma in your past?"

"No," she said. "I feel that if I took a break and moved out, it would be better; I'd be able to think of him more fondly. Isn't that strange? But I'm not going to leave. I'm an executive at Dior but, still, it's New York real estate. I'm not taking a new place and I don't want to inconvenience my friends. So how do I stay with him?"

"Forgiveness is a mystery, isn't it? But talk it out with James, and we'll figure it out here as well," Robert said.

II

That evening Catherine and James ordered in Chinese food for dinner and then they took a walk across 17th Street. They reached the Rubin Museum, where they stopped to look at a poster of a Tibetan Buddha in the window. When they returned home, she poured two glasses of Burgundy and they sat down in the living room.

"I've been having problems, James. I spoke about this with Robert, the therapist. Let's go over it. I need to get some things straight in my head," Catherine said.

"All right," James said.

"It's about the sex party. I didn't want to be there and you ignored me."

"I don't remember it that way," he said.

"How do you remember it?"

"We discussed, on the way, that it was new and it might feel strange but we wanted to try it. Do you recall that?"

"Yes," she said.

"When you said you weren't comfortable, I just thought you needed to give it some time."

"I don't know if I can get it out of my head that you left me and fucked that girl. Anyway, if it was supposed to help us sexually, wouldn't we have done it together?"

"Maybe there was something in the drinks," he said.

"There was definitely something in the drinks."

"We have to get over this," James said. He reached out for her hand and pulled her to him.

"No," she said, "Not now."

But the next night Catherine felt that their relationship was slipping away. I could walk out the door right now and never come back, she thought, and I'm not attracted to him at all.

She wanted to change things and make it better. James was watching TV on the sofa. Catherine stood over him, took the remote, turned off the TV, put her hand on his knee and said, "Go in the bedroom, take off your clothes, and lie down on your back."

James looked at her, wide-eyed, and, relieved, he rose and practically ran to the bedroom. Catherine waited a moment and then followed. She took off her jeans, shirt and panties and, leaving her bra on, climbed on top of him, straddled him and rubbed herself against him. He was immediately hard and she put him inside her. He reached to unhook her bra and she pushed his hands away and said, "I don't want you to touch me and I don't want you to look at me."

She moved up and down, and they were both turned on. Catherine found she loved dominating him and forbidding him to look at her, and for some reason it hit a deep chord in James as well. Catherine took her time and reached orgasm, and then she moved faster until James did.

Catherine lifted herself and walked out, instructing him to stay on the bed until she called for him. She went into the kitchen and sat down at the table. She thought, It worked for me to be in control, and it worked for him to be forced to look away. Why? She didn't know and felt she didn't need to. But as she leafed through a *Vanity Fair*, she thought, I still resent him.

She would have liked to talk about it with James, or with Robert for that matter, but after sex, she didn't know where to begin with James and as for Robert, he was on his summer break.

They were planning to visit a friend on Martha's Vineyard for two weeks, but Catherine didn't feel up to it and canceled.

She and James would spend the two weeks in town.

They took long walks along the West Side Highway and one day they picnicked on the Christopher Street Pier with ham and gruyere baguettes and a bottle of wine. They saw *The Avengers* and a Star Wars in the Union Square Theater, cooked vongole, beef bourguignon, and chicken in every way that a chicken could possibly be prepared: with white wine and capers, with rosemary and lemon, and with red sauce. They had a John Le Carré film festival in the living room, which included *The Night Manager*, *The Little Drummer Girl*, and *The Spy Who Came in from the Cold*, and they rewatched *The Sopranos* in its entirety.

Their sex life was at full force in its new iteration, as required by Catherine, with James being passive and looking away, and with her on top.

But by the second week, Catherine felt claustrophobic and suggested that they make plans with friends. James said, "No. You canceled the trip and we need it to be just us. We're working things out."

"We can't just be us," Catherine said.

"You mean if we were on an island together, we'd be unhappy?" he said.

"No one's on an island together and if they are, they just drink," Catherine said.

She looked in the mirror the next morning and thought, I'm not really dealing with the issue and I can't be with him for much longer. It will have to end.

On the last night before they went back to work, they cooked salmon with couscous.

James made a toast: "To us."

Catherine clicked her glass to him and smiled. But when James happened to look away—just as he was instructed to do when they were in bed—she shook her head.

III

Catherine had to travel for work and couldn't attend therapy at the beginning of September. James asked if he could go in her place and, since they'd started as a couple, Robert scheduled him in.

At the given hour, James sat down and gazed at Robert. Then he looked away, as if too shy to hold eye contact.

"How are things going, James?" Robert said.

"Good, I guess," James said. "A lot has happened since I met you that day. I imagine you've heard. We haven't been right since the night of the sex party in Chelsea, and I believe that Catherine's thinking of leaving me. We're fine on the surface, but she's distant. It feels like we cheated on each other at the orgy, and our sex life was dead. Now it's back but she resents me. I can feel it. The one thing I can tell you is this: We won't break up. I can't explain why."

"Can you try?" Robert said.

"No," James said, and then he crossed his arms and was silent.

Robert watched him and saw, in James, a man who was stuck.

Robert knew that he'd fallen into a conflict of interest: the sessions with each of them felt like separate therapies, and that wasn't sustainable. He thought, If it has to be therapy for one or the other, whom do I choose? Catherine? James?

He reminded himself that his decision shouldn't involve punishing James for his reticence—for James, sitting with his arms crossed, was reminding Robert of someone.

Himself.

□ □ □

Early in his career, Robert found women easier to treat than men. They tended to know what they were feeling when they were feeling it. Also, when his female patients would tell him a story, he could easily track how it related to why they were in treatment in the first place.

He'd experienced his male patients as being more opaque. They tended to intellectualize, and Robert would often strain to understand how their anecdotes related to their issues.

Years passed and the men who showed up for treatment seemed to be more emotionally intelligent than those who had come before. But this idea made Robert smile. He knew that the men hadn't changed. He had.

It was about his own stuff.

Robert remembered a moment with his father. For him, so much came back to that relationship.

When Robert was in his teens, his father always wanted him to wash the car and they'd argue. I must have been such a brat, he now thought, but he still specifically remembered one of those confrontations.

His father had said, "What are you even doing here?"

"In the house?"

"Yes," his father said.

"I live here," Robert said, and he'd stood his ground and crossed his arms.

Now he looked at James, who was silent and whose arms were crossed, and it all seemed familiar.

I just need more time with him, Robert thought.

IV

Catherine called to take the session the following week. She came in and Robert said, "Long time no see."

"Yes!" Catherine said. "The summer break, and then I had to travel for work. I guess I'm the only person in the world who doesn't like to spend two weeks in Paris! I like being home." Robert noted that she sometimes wore Dior to the sessions but other times, like today, was swearing a baggy sweater, jeans and moccasins.

"How are you two doing?" Robert said.

"Well, our sex life is back," she began. "A bit kinky, though ... You know, Robert, I've been having a recurring dream since the night of the party."

Robert looked at her.

"I'm with my uncle," she said. "I'm about seven years old and he's touching me sexually."

Robert waited and Catherine was silent.

He finally said, "With dreams, the questions I'd ask are two: First, what was the feeling?"

"Horror. Terror," she said. "He was running his hands up my leg. He touched me between my legs," and she stopped and covered her face with her hands. She slowly gathered herself and said, in a robotic voice, "Robert. What's the second question you ask about dreams?"

"The second question is: What are your associations?" he said.

She quietly said, "My associations? I don't know."

"What's he like, your uncle?"

She took a moment and she said, "He did it. That's what he's like."

"In real life?" Robert said.

"Yes. He did it," she said.

Robert felt his stomach tighten. He'd seen this so many times before. He quietly said, "I'm sorry, Catherine," and then, "We'll deal with this."

And that was what they tried to do. She came in for sessions for two months and James didn't. As she mulled over her memories of her uncle and the abuse, she suspected that she may have been violated more than once but she wasn't sure. Robert understood. That was what happened with abuse.

In some sessions, Catherine just cried. But one day she said, "You know, he colored everything in my life." She took out her phone and began to type and said, "I've been thinking about this all week. This is an email to everyone in my family," and she read: "Uncle Peter touched me sexually when I was seven."

"There, sent!" she said. "What do you think?"

She had done that so fast. Robert said, "I guess you did what you needed to do."

But the following week, Catherine reported that her uncle and everyone else had denied it ever happened, except her cousin Ronny, who said, "It was so long ago. Why don't you just put it behind you?" "Well, that makes things simple, doesn't it?" Catherine said. "I'm putting them in a time out. All of them. For now, I'm an orphan.

"By the way," she continued, "James wanted to drive to my uncle's home in Vermont and assault him. I told him no ... You know, James and I are tighter. I suppose I need him now, though I don't feel like having sex and he understands."

"I have a question," Robert said, "but if it's uncomfortable, feel free not to respond."

"Yes?" she said.

"Do you think the night in Chelsea triggered you, from what happened with your uncle?" Robert said.

"What do you mean?" she said.

"I mean it felt like a violation at the sex party, having sex when you didn't really want to. Did it trigger, deep down, the memory of your uncle, when you were violated? And do you think you're transferring that anger to James, even a little?"

Catherine took a moment and said, "Whatever. I need you to help me with James; a remedy."

"Time will help you with this, and our work will."

"But we're together every minute, Robert. I need something for today," she said.

"Today?"

She nodded and smiled.

"Hmm," Robert said, and he thought about it. "All right ... How's this? You wouldn't have been aware of the abuse if it had not been for James and the party."

"Huh?" she said.

"Let's assume that you needed to remember what happened with your uncle and to process it," Robert said. "Well, if not for James and that party, you might not have made it to therapy, and you might not have remembered it."

"And?" she said.

"Maybe that's part of the mystery of how people forgive," Robert said. "That the events of your life needed to take you to this moment, (a); and (b) you wouldn't have gotten there without James."

"So should I be grateful to him? Is that what you're saying?" Catherine said. "If I were raped, Robert, would I thank the rapist for helping me to remember something from my past? Are you joking?"

"No," Robert said, and he crossed his arms and tried again. "Letting your anger at James go, if that's ever possible for you, will be a lighter energy for you—whether you stay with him or not."

"So, can I find a way to be grateful to James that I slept with a stranger and realized that my uncle abused me?" She looked at him and said, "No, Robert. I can't."

V

"You heard about Catherine's uncle?" James said. He'd asked to come in for a session. "Did she tell you what I wanted to do?"

"Yes," Robert said.

"I hate bullies ... You know, Robert, I had a friend when I was a child. His name was Ray. I was ten," James said. "Ray was bullied by a group of boys in my neighborhood. He told me at the time how scared he was, and I was going to tell my parents or my teachers but I didn't. And then Ray died. He was riding his bicycle, fell off and hit his head. It was supposedly an accident but I knew it wasn't.

"I was questioned by the police. They suspected the boys, but I didn't say anything," James continued. "In any case, there probably wasn't enough evidence to convict them. But it has stayed with me all these years. I don't know why I'm telling you this. It's just that I hated those guys—and now, her uncle. How dare he do that to her?"

Robert said, "Do you think about it often?"

"Ray? Yes. I saw those guys in the cafeteria after Ray died, and I remember I smiled at them. I wanted them to like me, Robert." He took a deep breath. "I think about that a lot."

"What goes through your head when you think of it, James?"

"I was scared of them, I guess. But fear isn't an excuse."

"You were ten and fear wasn't an excuse?" Robert said.

James shook his head. "Enough. Isn't the world full of people who did what I did, in the face of bullies?"

"Yes, but—"

"I'm here about Catherine," James said. "She resents me because of her uncle, right?"

"Maybe," Robert said, and he sensed that James was seeking a moment of male solidarity. Two guys trying to hash things out, and the woman who had the problems, not the man.

James changed the subject, and they spent the rest of the time talking about his job. He worked in an ad agency and was having problems with his boss.

□ □ □

"James and I haven't been getting along," Catherine told Robert on the phone. "We think maybe you can help us. Can we come in for a couples session?"

"All right," Robert said, and it would be his last session with Catherine.

When they arrived, they each made eye contact with Robert but, he noticed, not with each other.

"I need to say something before we start," Robert said. "I've seen you both individually and I've seen you together as a couple, as we're doing today. It's OK to do a couples therapy and then to meet privately. But it feels that the private sessions have been much more than that, and those sessions need to go deeper."

"What are you saying?" Catherine said.

"We should figure this out. We can go on meeting for couples therapy, or I can treat one of you privately. I've been seeing you more, Catherine, and we've been discussing what happened with your uncle. We can keep doing that and I can refer James to a different therapist. Or I'll see James."

"So this is an ultimatum?" Catherine said and smiled.

"An admission of a miscalculation. A mistake on my part," Robert said.

"Who do you want to treat?" she said.

"It's not up to me," Robert said, and he thought, She experienced the sexual abuse and it's coming up in the sessions. I should treat her.

"Well, we're here now, so I'll start," Catherine said. Both men turned to her.

"James," she began. "Robert said some strange things: how my bad experience at the party brought out what my uncle did to me. I've been thinking about it all week. It's not the whole story but it's partly true. Sex triggers me. I had a boyfriend before you. We were starting to spend a lot of time together and I thought I loved him. One night we decided to move in together. We made love and I felt such repulsion afterward that I ended the relationship. I never understood that, but now I believe it may have had something to do with what happened with my uncle. And this may be the same thing. Maybe the night in Chelsea was about that. Partly."

"Catherine, you're saying your reaction to the night in Chelsea wasn't entirely about James, then?" Robert said.

"That's what I'm saying," Catherine said.

"Do you think you can forgive me?" James said.

"I can try," Catherine said.

"I just want us to stay together," James said, and then he said to Robert, "You know, being here has helped us figure these things out; that Catherine needs to deal with her stuff."

"You see that?" Catherine said to Robert with a derisive smile.

"What?" James said.

"What?" Robert said.

"Do you feel you have problems to deal with too, James?" Catherine said.

"Everyone has things to deal with," James said. "But I'm glad you're working on this. Maybe with Robert, you and him, alone."

Catherine raised her eyebrows. "Not so fast, James. And not so fast, both of you."

"What?" James said, and he and Robert turned to her.

"There are things we need to discuss besides my issues," Catherine said. "It's not all about me. I have a list, actually." She took out her phone, looked at it and then back at James, then at Robert.

"OK. So my parents came to New York last fall and James met them for the first time. You got drunk. Sloppily. You knew the meeting was important to me. Their opinion of you meant so much to me," and she turned to Robert: "At one point, he playfully slapped my father on the butt. Can you imagine that?" She turned back to James: "Why did you do that?"

"I drank too much," James said.

"Yes, but you knew what my family meant to me. I told you I wanted you to make a good impression and you sabotaged it. That's what you do, James. I've noticed."

"This sounds like it has to do with what happened with your family," James said.

"Robert's the shrink, not you," Catherine said. "And no, it's bigger. You have sabotage in you, can't you see that? I want to know why you sabotaged that first meeting with my parents?"

"I got drunk," James said.

"Well, I was embarrassed. I still am," Catherine said.

Robert said to Catherine, "Can James remedy this?"

"Well, he never apologized to them, or to me," she said.

"I'm sorry for getting drunk that day, Catherine," James said. "I can't really call your parents right now to apologize, can I, under the circumstances?"

"No, you don't need to call them," Catherine said. "That would be enough, but you always sabotage."

"That's crazy," James said.

She looked at her phone and then she said, "Then there's texting. I text him at work, he doesn't text back."

"I do," James said.

"Not fast enough," Catherine said. "It's as if he waits, Robert. As if he knows that I need a text back in a certain interval, say, in an hour, and it's as if he has a clock in his head. He waits two hours or three. I've spoken to him about this, but ... crickets."

"Doesn't that sound a bit paranoid?" James said, turning to Robert.

"I don't know," Robert said.

"Is the woman paranoid? Oh! Good question!" Catherine said. "Robert?"

"James should answer," Robert said.

"You don't believe me, Robert?" Catherine said.

"It's not about me," Robert said.

"Fine," Catherine said dismissively. "And then there's sex."

"What about sex? We don't have sex," James said.

"We had a system. We tried it and it worked. We don't need to go into that here."

"No, I'll go into it," James said. "It's non-movement on my part, non-eye contact."

"It worked for us," Catherine said. "My being in control. But when we've tried to have sex lately, he's been too rough. Twice. That's the opposite, the exact opposite, of what we were doing. I told him to stop and he didn't. Imagine being too rough with the girl who found out about her uncle."

"It's true," James said.

"Why do you think you did that, James?" Robert said.

"I told you why," Catherine said. "Sabotage."

"Let's remember that I'm the one who's committed in this relationship," James said. "I'm the one who wants it to work out. And when you talk about sabotage, it's not likely that it would be coming from me," James said.

Catherine looked from him to Robert.

"You see what's happening here?" Catherine said. "It's like the sex club in Chelsea. Sabotage. I didn't want to do it. We're not swingers. I'm not, at least."

"What are we even talking about?" James said. "You had a problem, your uncle. And I didn't know about your uncle at the time of the Chelsea party, and you didn't know about it, either."

"That's not good enough, James," Catherine said. "This session is over, thank God."

Robert looked at the clock and saw that the session had gone over time, and he knew that he had another patient arriving in five minutes.

"That's unfortunate, to end now," Robert said. "We can pick this up again. But on that, I need you to both let me know whether you want to come in as a couple, or whether I treat you privately, Catherine, or you, James."

"Not me," James said.

"Oh, I'm sure not you! You're problem-free. I'm the sick one. What do you think, Robert?" Catherine said.

"I think you and I can work privately, Catherine. We can work through the sexual violation."

"It's not the woman who's always crazy," Catherine said to Robert. And the session ended.

Robert didn't hear from them after that. He left voice messages.

A month passed and then another.

At that point, not having received a reply, he thought, I didn't know which one I was treating, and in the last session, Catherine thought I was siding with James. This made Robert wince. He knew they weren't likely to come back.

He thought, Well, Catherine uncovered a childhood trauma in the treatment. Even if we don't meet again, she can pick up the issue when she's ready, with someone else.

And as for James? He had issues as well, Robert thought, regretfully. We never really dealt with those.

VI

The following March, on a Sunday, Robert was in the Metropolitan Museum of Art, in a sprawling, baroque gallery. The enormous room was packed with perhaps seventy people. He was enjoying himself and getting lost in the paintings; they took him far away from his everyday life. Then he spotted Catherine. She was with a man, and Robert was able to see the man's profile, and that it wasn't James.

He moved to say hello but stopped himself. He and Catherine weren't friends, after all. He'd merely been a professional in her life. She had a right to her privacy.

He turned to walk away but, again, he paused. He couldn't help but think of the singularity of the moment and of his job. He knew Catherine intimately: he knew what her uncle had done to her when she was a little girl, and probably done to her several times, and he remembered the way her face looked when she discovered that. He knew the way she liked to have sex with her boyfriend. But now she was just another well-heeled woman in the Met, suddenly a stranger, to whom he wouldn't even say hello.

He thought, When you've seen so intimate a side of someone, when they've trusted you that much, you care for them. I'd like to know if she's all right, and maybe have her know me a little bit, too.

He stood there, pondering this.

What occurred to him next—and he realized that this wouldn't cross the minds of the vast majority of men in the Met that day—was that at least a quarter of the women in the museum and in the gallery, the New York women and the tourists, those with black hair, blond, red and brunette, curly and straight, those who were Black, White, and Asian, those in dresses, skirts, and jeans, those wearing glasses and those without, and probably closer to half of them, actually, when you factor in those who'd remained silent, and so many fewer of the men, had endured some form of sexual abuse in their childhoods or their young adulthoods. It was a statistic, numbers on a page, and in that sense, it was almost beyond comprehension—but it rang true to him: he'd seen the effects with Catherine and in so many other patients; some of them men, many of them, women.

But the women in the gallery that day, and the men, just carried on. It was just another Sunday afternoon in New York.

He shook his head, took a deep breath and looked back at Catherine for the last time. She was tightly holding the arm of the man she was with, in their winter coats. They were looking up at Ruben's *Venus and Adonis* together and smiling.

She seemed happy. Robert basked in that for a moment. Then he turned and left.

□ □ □

In the spring a year later, James phoned and asked to come in for a private session. Robert scheduled him in for the first week in May.

When James arrived, he seemed more tentative than before, and his shoulders were slumped. He sat down and said, "I should tell you. Catherine broke up with me. Seems like ages ago. We're done."

"What happened?" Robert said.

"She kept accusing me of sabotage," James said. "She said I sabotage everything, do you remember? I blamed her uncle and she couldn't stand that either, and one day she just moved out. She stayed with a friend, and that was it. I was devastated."

"I'm sorry," Robert said.

"I tried to get her to reconsider. I called, then I stopped by her friend's but, well, when she makes up her mind, she's done … I was going to come back and see you sooner, but I didn't know if it would make a difference," James said. "I thought I just needed to deal with it and a lot of it was my fault, Robert, I know that. So I toughed it out. I didn't eat, I lost weight, but I got through it. At least, well enough."

"That's good, James," Robert said.

"You might think this is crazy, Robert. But I didn't come back here to talk about Catherine. Not at all. Maybe it seems fast to you, it's been a year, but there's a woman at work, a good friend, Jodie's her name, and we've known each other for a long time. After Catherine left, she saw what I was going through and invited me out for a drink. She really knows how to listen. Then we started to go out more regularly. I thought we were friends. We went out for food on MacDougal Street, to bars and, well, I'm seeing her now. After all this time, we've gotten serious. That's why I'm here. I don't want to make the same mistakes as I did with Catherine."

"Why don't you tell me what's going on?" Robert said.

"OK. So, Jodie texts me when I'm out, and I notice that I don't text back right away," he said. "Do you remember that Catherine accused me of not texting her back? I thought she was just being paranoid but I realize, Robert, that it's as if I have a clock in my head, just as Catherine said. I wait and wait. But Jodie wants to hear from me. She's made that very clear. Do you know that I have to actually force myself to text back in a timely way? And I do, Robert. I force myself."

"Good," Robert said.

"Not only that. I met Jodie's parents and I was careful not to drink too much. I really wanted to drink more, but I didn't want to embarrass her. I didn't want to make that mistake twice. Do you remember I was drunk when I met Catherine's parents?"

"I remember," Robert said.

"And I'm careful sexually, too. Not too rough. I won't do that again."

Robert nodded.

"When Catherine left me—" James began, but then he said, "I care for Jodie, Robert, but she's not Catherine," and he laughed. "And I didn't want to talk about Catherine today! She's all I'm talking about, I think."

"You're talking about yourself," Robert said.

"Right," James said. "So, perhaps one day I'll care for Jodie as much as I cared for Catherine. But I've had time to think, Robert. Here's the thing: I was pushing Catherine to stay with me. That was what I said on the first day of couples therapy. Remember? We can't break up; that you, Robert, can't break us up. And then I was like John Cusack in that movie, showing up at her friend's apartment. I had everything but the boom box to hold up to her window! But now I know that aside from whatever happened with her uncle, I did all those things she said I did. I don't know if I really wanted to sabotage us, but I ended up doing it."

"Can you explain some more?" Robert said.

"When you push someone to stay together the way I did, maybe I pushed her away," James said.

"The pushing thing you're talking about, and what you did, we can deal with those types of things here, James," Robert said. "We can knock it out and pretty fast, too. But not as a one-off."

"No, Robert," James said.

"You know, James, I made a mistake when I was seeing you and Catherine. We juggled between private sessions and couples sessions. It was a bad situation," Robert said.

"She learned about her uncle with you," James said. His eyes became moist. "Robert. I just needed to run the Jodie thing by you. I needed to tell you what I did with Catherine that I don't want to do again."

"I see. It's OK, James, but—"

"I'm not up for more than that with you," James said and he stood. "Hey, Robert! Remember the first time we came in, Catherine and I? I left after five minutes. I stormed out. And now I'm saying I won't continue in treatment again. I guess some things never change!" and he rolled his eyes and smiled.

"Right," Robert said, and he tried to smile back.

"I'm going to leave now," James said.

"We have more time, James," Robert said. "You can at least take the whole session."

"I don't need it," James said. "Well, there is one more thing, I guess."

"Yes?"

James sat back down. "I've thought about a session we had, just the two of us. Do you remember? I told you about a boy, Ray?"

"I remember."

"I know you're a good therapist because you were kind to me that day. You didn't judge me, but, um, you were wrong, Robert."

"How so?" Robert said.

"I could have saved a boy's life when I was ten and I didn't," James said.

"That might be true, but—"

"No buts," James said. "People get bullied all the time and I said they deal with it, and you agreed. But you needed to see it the other way, Robert."

"Which way?" Robert said.

"That my behavior was unforgivable," James said.

"We spoke about this, James. You were ten," Robert said.

"It doesn't matter," James said. Then, after a moment, he said, "It's funny: do you remember how Catherine and I had sex? She made me lie down and not look at her? No eye contact? It's as if she knew, Robert! But I never told her about Ray. And, well, I guess she did it for her own reasons. It was about her uncle, right?"

Robert was trying to fathom all that James was intimating, but before he could gather himself and speak, James stood again and walked to the door.

"You and I, Robert. We're good," James said.

"Are you sure you don't want to—"

"Don't worry about me and don't worry about whatever you think you did wrong. Catherine was in pain. I know that," James said.

"You're leaving?" Robert said, and he spoke quickly. "All right. But before you go, just know, James, you can always come back, anytime. I'm here."

"Thank you, Robert," James said, and he left and closed the door behind him.

Robert sat for a moment, discombobulated, and then he turned on his laptop to take session notes but he couldn't. He was crying. He wiped his eyes.

He made himself type: James is unforgivable to himself, and he added: so far.

Robert's mind drifted and he thought of how Catherine had made James look away during sex. How amazing. It was as if she knew about his shame with Ray but she didn't. She'd done it for her own reasons, as James had said. He marveled at how people are drawn together by forces they don't understand. The roots are so deep. And the same, as far as how people get together sexually and what turns them on in bed.

He thought, Perhaps James will return.

I'll be here.

I'll be ready.

Robert stood, walked to the window, and stared out at the antique store across the street. He saw the stone Buddha on display there. He remembered he'd noticed it long before with Catherine, but back then the Buddha had seemed severe, off-putting, even reticent. It had reminded him, incongruously, of this: an unhappy teen sitting in a chair with his arms crossed, and silent.

But now it had changed. The owners of the shop had since placed a blue-topaz necklace set in silver around the Buddha's neck, and it draped down on its dark-gray chest. The blue topaz played off the stone and beautified the Buddha. Robert stared at it for a few minutes. The necklace rendered a similar effect, Robert imagined, as if the Buddha were holding a bouquet of violets.

RECONSTRUCTIONS

(Paul)

I

Robert had been a New Yorker at the time of 9/11, but he'd lived uptown. As New Yorkers would say: To the world, America was attacked, to America, New York was attacked, and to New Yorkers, downtown was attacked. Indeed, in the weeks after 9/11, the restaurants in his neighborhood on the Upper East Side were in full swing, but he knew that life downtown was different. Those who lived there had experienced the tragedy firsthand, and Robert would learn about what it was like when Paul, forty-five, came in for his first session.

"I've been thinking of 9/11," he began. "I'm at a point where I need to deal with it. It hit me on the anniversary this week, all these years later."

"Do you have an idea of why it hit you this year in particular?" Robert said, as he did the math in his head; it was seventeen years past.

"It's about my boyfriend, Richard."

"Did you lose him in 9/11?"

"No. More recently."

"Did he die?"

"He left me but I died," Paul said.

"What do you mean?" Robert said.

"I mean when someone you love dies to you, don't you think you die a little as well?" Paul said.

"Could be," Robert said.

"That's what I'm saying. I'm a ghost."

"Can you describe what happened on 9/11 or with your boyfriend?" Robert said.

"No, I don't want to. Not yet."

"All right."

"You're asking very direct questions," Paul said. "I don't know if you'll get real answers from people with such questions."

"I'm just trying to get a sense of who you are. Maybe you want to ask me something?" Robert said.

"Can you talk to me about death?" Paul said.

Robert took a moment.

He was aware of the analytic theory: that anything he would say about his personal life and beliefs, such as about death, might bias or inhibit his new patient. But Robert gave himself a wide berth in this regard.

Why? For one thing, while Freud preached that analysts needed not to self-disclose and to be blank slates to their patients, Robert wasn't an analyst and it was common knowledge that on occasion, Freud invited patients to spend the summer with him and his family. But more than that, Robert saw psychotherapy as an art, not a science, and understood that there was a random, even magical element to it. He regarded relevant self-disclosure as an artist might—one who puts a color on a canvas because of an intuition she can't quite explain or justify, but it ends up enhancing the painting. He sometimes found that things he revealed would land with his patients in ways that neither he nor they could anticipate, and would often be pivotal for the treatment.

The fact was, Paul asked what Robert thought of death and Robert had been through a significant death recently. Not to answer truthfully, Robert felt, would be a sort of manipulation by omission.

"It's a big subject, what I think of death," Robert finally said. "My father died last year."

"Oh? I'm sorry."

"He was ready to go," Robert said. "He'd had it. He was on oxygen for months. He couldn't walk anymore."

"How old was he?"

"Eighty-eight."

"So it was easier for you than my loss was for me," Paul said.

"Perhaps," Robert said. "Why don't you tell me about you and Richard? Would that be a good idea?"

"All right. But you still owe me one."

"I owe you one?" Robert said.

"About death," Paul said.

Robert laughed and said, "All right."

"You want to know about Richard and me? Let's see," Paul said. "Well, he was my professor at Columbia. We're architects, by the way. He's renowned. I was his student, though not an ordinary one. I'm good at what I do, so you could say that I was his prized student. And Richard, Ritchie Rich, I always called him, is a working architect. He taught at Columbia just to, um, mentor youth," and he laughed.

"What's funny about that?"

"Richard was eighteen years my senior. That was always an issue for him. It's why he left me, ultimately. Anyway, he saw my talent and asked me out for a drink one night. Keep in mind, I was in awe of him and of the buildings he'd done. But I also had a crush. Maybe I have father issues, I don't know. What do you think happens after death? after things end? That's important to me."

"You're telling a good story here."

"But I need to know who I'm dealing with."

"All right." Robert paused for a moment and then he said, "I'll tell you a story from my life, Paul. It's symbolic, about death. It's a bit involved, though."

"I'd like to hear it."

"OK ... I once had a friend," Robert began, hoping his story wouldn't take them too far off-track. "He was my best friend, Graham was his name, and I thought we'd be as close as two friends could possibly be, for life. We joked about that, that when we'd be old, we'd be sitting on a porch somewhere, chatting away. We met when we worked together, early on;

I was in real estate for a year or two. And then one day he stopped being my friend. Like that. He didn't explain why. He just blocked me everywhere.

"I tried to figure it out for years," Robert continued. "I asked myself what I'd done wrong. I went through all the offhand things that may have offended him. What were they? One day I'd run into his wife in town and we'd had coffee. Did I flirt with her? I wondered. Maybe. But we were all old friends at that point. What else? He used to make jokes about his job in real estate and I'd laugh along with him and I'd add to the jokes. Did I come off as too critical? Could be. The odd thing to me, now, is that I never asked him what had happened. I can't imagine how I never confronted him. It's not like me not to, but I didn't. And after a few years I realized I had no answers and I'd never have any. He was just gone. The friendship was over.

"I grieved ... I battled it in my head for maybe a decade. Not a crying type of grieving, but it just kept coming back to me, while driving, taking a walk, reading; a why-did-he-go?-type thing. What did I do wrong? But eventually I got over it. And do you know what I came up with?"

"What?" Paul said.

"Things die. Friendships die. And sometimes they die before we do. And maybe that's the natural order of things."

"What do you mean?" Paul said.

"I mean, when we die all of our friendships are over anyway, right?" Robert said. "But before that, when we get old, we lose track of people. I saw that with my parents as they aged. So maybe that's what life and death really are, symbolically. Things die before we do, and that's OK. Because the people are still with us, in a way, in our minds, in our histories. But the actual connection itself lives and dies, so no need to be greedy and require that our actual relationships last forever."

Paul nodded and said, "I'd like you to be my therapist."

"You would? Well, I'd like to be," Robert said. "Thank you. I'm glad."

Paul looked at him. "So what now?"

"Can you tell me about you and Richard?"

"Well, this was all triggered by the 9/11 anniversary, so I'll tell you a story," Paul said, and he sat up straighter.

"In 2001, Richard took a wine course at Windows on the World," he began. "I'd pick him up every Tuesday night. Do you know the World Trade Towers had a somewhat small, semi-circular driveway on the West Side Highway? It was so funny in scale, as if it were a driveway to a good-sized house or a small mansion. So I'd drive there in Richard's convertible to pick him up at ten o'clock, after class. I'd park there, top down, it was late April, early May, that first rush of spring, and I'd look up at the towers. They were especially enormous from that perspective. Two straight vertical shots. You know, I never thought they were attractive, the World Trade Towers. Did you?"

"Not especially," Robert said.

"I found them horrible from an architectural standpoint. We could see them from our living room window. They were like two middle fingers saying fuck you, and they were not at all connected to the landscape. I'd look at them and imagine that if there were as big a jump forward in time as there was between, say, us and the dinosaurs, if you had a *Planet of the Apes*-type thing and the society had crumbled, someone would still discover those steel towers, eons later. They'd still be there, in some form. And I thought, They shouldn't be.

"But, you know, at dawn they were better," Paul said. "The steel caught a silver light from the sky, and they looked beautiful then, but gently so; gleaming. They were a part of my mornings when I'd have coffee in our dining room. And at night, they were different, too. The maintenance services cleaned and people worked late; the lights were on, the steel disappeared and they became luminous. The towers turned into one hundred ten floors of amber lights. They were beautiful then, too. Alluring.

"Anyway, on a Tuesday night in April, I was in the driveway of the World Trade Towers waiting for Richard, and I was looking up and I was thinking, this moment is perfect. The two towers of amber lights were beautiful, I loved Richard, he was about to come out and we'd go to dinner, and I thought, We'll have a civil union, we'll stay together, and this moment will endure. Nothing will ever change.

"Just then, two older couples came out of the revolving doors. They'd obviously had dinner at Windows on the World and they were old-fashioned glamorous, the men in long coats, their wives dressed impeccably—one with her hair up. And I looked at them and I remembered thinking: This is too

Gatsby; something's gotta give. My life is too good right now, and their lives are. You know, America was flying so high in those days, after the '90s.

"And as I watched those couples—urbane is the word I'd use to describe them—I thought, Well, what will give is they won't be here forever. They were probably in their seventies. I thought, They'll die at some point. That's what will give. And my mind went from there to thinking about Richard. I mean, he was only in his late forties but we had an age difference. It was a bigger deal for him than it was for me. But the thought did cross my mind: I'll outlive him, which I knew early on, but I'd put it out of my mind. And that's what will give, I thought, that's what will change and end.

"I tried to prepare for my outliving Richard when we met, three years before the wine class," he continued. "I want to jump around in my story. Is that all right?"

"Yes," Robert said.

"OK, so. Three years before, he was my professor. I told you. Once, after class, we went out for a drink. And that first night, we went to the top of the Empire State Building. Nothing much came of it, we kissed, but after the semester ended, he called me and we went out again, and then we slept together. That night, he became so ridiculous. It was very funny."

"How so?" Robert said.

"In bed, Richard said he thought that being with a younger person, an ex-student, was inappropriate." Paul laughed. "He told me about this couple he knew at One Fifth, a gay couple.

They'd met when they were probably the ages we were then, the younger man in his twenties or early thirties, the older one in his late forties, early fifties. He knew them and he'd see them together in the street. He said that the older man was now in his nineties, hunched over on a walker, and the younger man was still spry, in his late sixties. And Richard said he thought the younger man was burdened with the older one, even if they still loved each other. He said, 'It would be humiliating to be with a younger person and have him watch me get older.' That was so funny to me and I laughed out loud, because he was saying he cared for me and wanted to be with me, right? It was the first time we slept together! So I turned to him and said, 'You love me already!' 'No!' he said. 'Exactly,' I said, 'You don't even know me, Richard.' But I was thrilled, not thinking that he loved me, exactly, but thinking he was taking me more seriously than he'd intended.

"We kept seeing each other," Paul said. "We'd have dinners and I'd stay over. The age difference was strange for me too, you know? I thought, He won't be with me forever. It was a dull feeling, but for later; easy to put aside. And then we went through a phase where he wanted to buy me!" Paul laughed again.

"What do you mean?" Robert said.

"He offered to pay for my school. I said no," Paul said. "Then he offered to subsidize my rent. Anything for him to feel he didn't have to be all in. I didn't take him up on any of it. Instead, one day I showed up at his apartment with my stuff. I'd been spending more and more time there and I had a key at that point. I hid the bags in the second bedroom. When he got home that night, I'd cooked vongole and lit candles, and at dinner I said, 'We have a lot to celebrate, Richard.' He said, 'Yes, we do.' We toasted each other, and then he raised his eyebrows and he said, quite casually, 'What would that be, that we're celebrating?' and I said, 'I moved in! I live here now!' You should have seen his eyes. The pure shock! The unadulterated terror! But that was it. We were together after that."

Paul lost himself in the memory, with a faraway smile, but then his expression changed and his eyes began to well up. As Robert watched, Paul gathered himself and held back his tears.

"Where was I? I was telling you a different story," Paul said. "Three years later, when Richard was taking a wine course at Windows on the World; I'd pick him up on Tuesday evenings ... I'd wait for him in the driveway in his car. Then at ten, he'd come down and we'd go out to dinner—often on Clinton Street. There was a little place called Clinton Fresh. We'd go there or to some other little chic spot. It was very romantic."

Paul took a deep breath.

"Richard's wine class ended in June and then, of course, September came, and 9/11. That's another story for another day. I know we're running out of time," and they both turned and looked at the clock on Robert's side table. They had five more minutes.

"But the towers fell in September. And after they did, after all of the trauma we went through, after the nightmare of that time, and all the craziness and all the sirens, one day I remembered back to that spring evening, back to when I picked Richard up after the wine class. Back to when life had still been normal. And I recalled the two older couples coming out of the lobby, all dressed up, and how I'd thought, Something had to give. And it occurred to me: Well, it did. But could I have ever dreamed it wouldn't be the two older couples who might die, or Richard who might, but the towers! The actual buildings that would fall?

"I mean, we're Americans, right?" he continued. "The country that built big things. Skyscrapers. Suspension bridges ..."

His eyes became moist again.

"What does that story bring up for you, Paul?" Robert said.

"If the buildings can disappear in an instant, if two steel towers, one hundred ten floors can just be erased and become ghosts, then all bets are off, right?"

"How so?" Robert said.

"Then breakups are real. Then death is real."

□ □ □

Death is real?

After the session, Robert thought about what Paul said and he asked himself, is it really?

Robert prayed and meditated regularly, and he thought those practices affected his temperament and even marked his identity. I'm a meditating-type guy, he felt. And indeed, when his father died earlier that year, the prayer and meditation had apparently paid off, because his father's passing hadn't really thrown him. And wasn't that a fundamental goal of looking within, to be less fearful of change and death? To him it seemed so, but he'd felt so little disruption after his father's passing that, now, after the session with Paul, he wondered if his reaction should be of concern.

His father, a man who loved life, had been going downhill for a long time. He'd been an avid golfer, but for the final two years of his life, he hadn't been able to walk without a walker. For the last six months, he was on prophylactic oxygen at home. And in the final month, he stopping drinking, which was, for him, truly the last straw: he loved having a few drinks at night.

Then, finally, he fell and broke his leg. The subsequent operation, and the anesthesia it required, marked the beginning of the end. He never left the hospital.

Robert reflected how he and his father always had a tempestuous relationship and it had tormented Robert early on in life. Still, he loved his father and, in the last year of his father's life, he began to prepare the eulogy for the day that he knew was fast approaching. He worried that he'd be on the podium at his father's funeral and he'd be caught empty-handed, and only remember their past difficulties. He wanted, instead, to stand up for him, and to give an account of his father's positive attributes, of which there were many.

What else went through Robert's mind? He remembered that he did cry for his father, near the end. His father was on a ventilator and Robert knew that his time wasn't long. He'd turned away from his father's hospital bed and sobbed.

But now, before his next session, he asked himself, how many patients have I helped through the death of a mother or a father? So many. Yet how is it that the death of my own father didn't really throw me at all?

□ □ □

Robert found it fascinating that Paul, an architect, had lost Richard and was relating it to buildings and 9/11. He wanted to learn more about Richard and he decided to google him.

Robert took out his phone and entered: Richard, Columbia University, architect, professor, but he hesitated. He'd looked up people before, but generally he preferred to learn about his patients' worlds through their own eyes. He put away his phone.

In their next session, when Paul was silent for the first two minutes, Robert jumped right in.

"You said that if the buildings fell, then breakups are real. What does that mean to you, Paul?" he said.

"What does it mean?" Paul said. "That we like to think that something survives when things end. Buildings expire and they get torn down but then they're rebuilt, right? Like death, and then new life. But in this case, they just vanished.

The World Trade Towers were just erased. Richard left me, but it feels strange to think he's gone forever. Do you believe he is?"

"Why don't you tell me about the relationship?" Robert said.

"I will," Paul said, but his tone of voice belied his words. "Would you tell me about grieving? Psychologically? I've been wondering about that."

"Grieving? All right," Robert said, and he took a deep breath. "Our understanding of it has changed, Paul. We used to think that the idea was to eventually leave the loss behind, just as a child leaves behind the clothes he's outgrown. But now we think that some people may not need to move beyond a loss and they don't necessarily have to."

"So Richard can still be my boyfriend?"

"Well, you're talking about a breakup and I think that's different."

"But grieving's the same, no?" Paul said.

"Can you tell me more about Richard?"

Paul was silent.

"Do you feel you've been grieving the loss of the relationship?" Robert said.

"I miss Richard," Paul said, "but I've been kind of numb. But then, the 9/11 anniversary happened and I realized that just as the buildings had disappeared, I had, too. I've been a shadow of myself. I was going to tell you about that."

"The anniversary?" Robert said.

"No. I need to go back to the event itself."

II

"So it was, I don't know, three months after Richard's wine class ended," Paul began in the next session and he sat back in his chair. "I was in our living room one morning, Richard was in the bedroom, he was watching NY1, and he said that a plane had hit the World Trade Towers. He saw it first on TV." Paul smiled ironically. "Isn't that perfect? We were a mile away and he saw it on TV.

"So I went to the living room window and I was looking at the hit tower. The bended steel. It was amazing in a gruesome sort of way," he continued. "And a half-hour later, I was still there and Richard was there with me when the other plane hit. I don't remember actually seeing the second plane itself. Maybe I was looking down or away. But I heard a big noise, looked up, and I saw the fireball. It was a magnificent sight. It was the most beautiful morning, San Diego weather, in the sixties, a blue sky, and I looked up and saw a golden fireball that looked to be ten floors in its span. And then it was gone. In the course of three seconds. And you see something like that and you say to yourself, were my eyes playing a trick? Did it really happen? Because it was like an apparition, a magician's illusion of fire.

"Then, well, we went through hell, living downtown," he said. "It's as if bin Laden attacked us personally. He attacked Richard and me. But here's the thing: we dealt with it in real time."

Robert nodded and Paul continued.

"You know, when I was little, I remember my father once took me into the ocean," he said. "I'd just learned to swim and we were jumping these big waves. He was holding my hand and when waves came that were too big to jump, he said, calmly, hold your breath and we'll go under them. And we did it. Like that. There was no time to be scared.

"9/11 was like that. That day and in the weeks and months that followed, there were sirens and police tearing through the streets that were closed down. The stench of the fires, the stench of the bodies and, I don't know, the fax machines were all in the air. But we dealt with it and we got over it.

"But then I was seeing the replays on TV," he said. "And I understood that Osama had attacked Richard and me and our neighbors, but the real terrorism was more self-imposed, more ... electronic. This was where the real fear was generated. I truly think that people in St. Louis or Phoenix had a worse time of 9/11 than Richard and I did, and we lived through it. It was a mile away. We just jumped under the waves, so to speak. Kept going ... I remember I'd take these baths with some strange salts I bought in a store on First Avenue. I don't remember the name of those, but it was said that they'd draw the poisons out of my skin. Anyway, as I got over the event—as *we* did, in two, three months—the fear seemed to exacerbate for the rest of the country. And when I watched it repeat and repeat on TV, my dread was worse from the TV version than it had been from the real version. The fireball was awe-inspiring in person, magnificent in a strange way, but not frightening. But seeing it over and over on TV? That's when I got scared in a bigger way than I ever did on 9/11."

He stared at Robert for a moment. Then he continued.

"Richard and I didn't see the towers actually fall," he said. "He'd fractured his shoulder and we had to go to see Dr. Nicholas, an orthopedic surgeon uptown. We called a car while the World Trade Towers were burning and then we went down to make the appointment, as if life were still normal. An old Israeli driver picked us up in the car service. He just shook his head and said, in a thick accent, 'I've seen this before.'

"We went to the doctor and by the time we returned home, there were no towers anymore," Paul said. "They'd fallen. And somehow, it wasn't real for me, those two towers just ... missing. Maybe when those buildings fell, something shifted."

"In you?" Robert said.

"In my concept of buildings, for one thing. Do you know Richard and I kissed for the first time on the top of the Empire State Building? Remember? I told you. It was while I was still his student, before we were dating, we went out for a drink, and afterward I told him I'd never been up there, and we went. When we were on the viewing deck he was pointing out the sights, and we were looking at the Woolworth Building, the World Trade Towers and of course, the Chrysler, and there were all these tourists, and then I kissed him. He was shy, kind of a gay-generational bashfulness, and we were making out. He was very self-conscious.

"Anyway, since that day, when I look at the Empire State Building, I think of that kiss," he said. "I think of Richard. So the building is not itself anymore, it's become something new for me. How do you grieve when you can't look at the Empire State Building? It's always there. You just have to look up in midtown. I think about that: What do buildings mean over time?"

"That's interesting."

"Yes. You know, I'm as well-known an architect as Richard was when we met. I am, thanks mostly to his mentoring and help. And when I think of new buildings, say, I recently renovated an apartment for a young couple in Flatiron. I tried to take them into account, thinking of how they'd live in the space, and this led me to think of the next generation after them. It occurred to me: Maybe the future people won't have love stories of the same order. Maybe their lives won't be destined to have happy endings, so to speak, as we always supposed; not the same upward trends. No Beatles 'love, love, love,' no U2, or whatever version your generation thinks that love is."

"I'm not sure I follow, Paul," Robert said.

"Sorry. My thoughts are scattered. Here it is: The Beatles, U2, the Empire State Building, those were frames of reference. But what about when we arrived home from

Dr. Nicholas and there was a blank space out our window where the World Trade Towers used to be? What then? The towers became ghosts. And this country did too, no? Maybe it started on that day, on 9/11."

"How so?" Robert said.

"Come on," Paul said. "When I graduated, I paid off my loans in a few years, but the numbers have changed. Now it's as if these kids spend enough on education to buy a house but without getting the house; just the bill. They don't have real health care. Or take the fire drills. Tell me, Robert: if I were building a school, would I design bullet-proof shelters for the eight-year-olds? And would those be of a different size than the ones I'd design for the five-year-olds? You see, this country isn't itself anymore. That's what happened after 9/11."

"Maybe. But there are never just ghosts, Paul," Robert said. "There's always more to it. But why don't we talk about you and Richard?"

"There are never just ghosts? What do you mean by that?" Paul said.

"I mean there are always psychological reasons for everything," Robert said. "Our enemies had psychological reasons to attack us on 9/11. Maybe it was about America's role in the Muslim world or maybe it was a tactic, an asymmetrical form of combat. And people have their own psychological reasons to retreat into themselves. To become ghosts. There are payoffs."

"Such as?" Paul said.

"Being a victim can be a payoff. Being a part of a tribe is a payoff."

"Can you explain?" Paul said.

"I can, Paul," Robert said. "We can discuss politics all you want, but would you mind if we talked about you first?"

"All right," Paul said.

"Why do you feel like a ghost? Can you say anything about that, or about Richard?"

Paul stared at Robert and then he spoke: "I'm not ready to talk more about Richard at this point. Anyway, I did talk to you about him. I've said a lot already."

"Then can we talk about you?" Robert said.

"If you like. Then I'll ask you this: What do you do if it's too late for someone, Robert? What does a therapist do?"

"That's complicated."

"Then uncomplicate it. Let's say you were the therapist on the *Titanic*. The ship's going down and I come to you and I say, 'I'm apprehensive about my future. Frankly, I don't think I'm going to have one.' Would you say, 'Why don't you tell me about your mother?'"

"No, I wouldn't, but—"

"I don't know how to process this loss of Richard. I can't."

Robert let Paul's words wash over him and then he said, "We'll figure that out, Paul, how to process this, together."

"All right," Paul said. "Because I think I went down with those buildings on 9/11."

"How so?"

Paul looked at the clock and said, "We're out of time. I guess I have to go. But before I do, would you tell me that story again?"

"Which one?"

"About your friend who stopped being your friend?"

"Sure," Robert said.

Paul sat back and he looked up at the ceiling, his head on the back of the chair.

"He cut me off after years of friendship," Robert began. "My best friend."

"You thought you were going to be friends for life?" Paul said.

"I did, and I was so hurt."

"And you never asked him why he did it?"

"No," Robert said, "and that's not like me. I just let it go. But I twisted and turned and I suffered, and I tried to understand it. I made up all these reasons. And what I finally came up with was this: maybe some things aren't made to last forever."

"So you're not bitter?" Paul said.

"No," Robert said. "I arrived at a place where I was happy for what we had. It was a good friendship. It didn't have to last forever. I felt it had lived out its life span. It's like having cut flowers in your house. They have a life span."

"And that's real to you?" Paul said.

"Yes."

"All right," Paul said sadly. Then he rose and walked slowly out of the office.

III

The treatment with Paul is affecting me, Robert thought, perhaps as much as it is affecting my patient.

The question lingered in his mind: Was it really that easy for me, losing Graham? Was that all true, what I said?

As far as that particular friendship was concerned, he concluded, it definitely was. He'd been tormented by the loss for years but he'd come to a peaceful place with it, as he'd said.

Robert practiced hot yoga twice a week and the next day, in class, he asked himself the same question—is what I'm telling myself true?—but this time, regarding his father.

Often in hot yoga, Robert would mentally recite the eulogy he'd given at his father's funeral, which had come off well at the ceremony. His yoga friends in the Wednesday morning class, two married women in their forties, Donna and Lorenza, would never suspect that on some days he silently intoned his father's eulogy in its entirety. Doing so took his mind off the 102-degree heat, but more essentially, it was his form of grieving. And on this day, he found himself doing it again.

As he joined his hands over his head, pointed his index fingers to the ceiling and leaned his head straight back, he reached the point of the eulogy when he'd met his father for dinner. It reverberated in his mind:

The dinner was at an Italian place he loved, in Murray Hill. I'd arrived late and I was visibly distraught. My father said, "What's wrong?" and I said, "It's a patient, Dad. She's having a hard time." He thought for a moment and he said, "Call her. Invite her to join us."

Robert remembered how the story had elicited knowing grins from all of the mourners at his father's funeral. Everyone knew about his father's remarkable generosity. But the story went on, for Robert, in yoga class:

My father thought for a moment and then he added, "In fact, Robert. If you ever want to invite any of your patients to dinner, no need to ask me in advance. Just bring them." And I said, "Dad, it doesn't work that way, but thank you."

Robert paused in his interior monologue.

He reflected that in addition to his father's generosity, the story illustrated his father's abundant compassion—but now he thought, Wasn't it also about my father's naivete and a lack of boundaries? But overanalyzing was a therapist's occupational hazard, and Robert decided to bask in those first two qualities of his father's personality: generosity and compassion.

He watched Donna and Lorenza, in their yoga shorts and halter tops, pin-wheeling their bodies to the floor, and he did as well.

He reflected how his father had played such a big role in making him who he was. But now, it seemed to Robert, he needed to review the relationship because, at that moment, in yoga, he couldn't feel his father at all. The older man was like the towers, which had just disappeared.

He wondered who his father was to him now? Was he just gone forever?

Then Robert thought of the phone call he'd received from his sister, Suzanne, earlier in the week. She'd told him that she was thinking of issuing a complaint to the president of the hospital. It concerned the way the nurses had behaved the day his father died. And this led Robert to mentally cast aside the eulogy and now, as he sweated in front of the mirror with thirty other people, to think about his father's last days, and his death.

He'd had a living will and years before, he'd named Robert to be his health-care proxy. "I know that if it's called for, you'll let me go," his father had said. In other words, his father trusted that Robert would pull the plug if all hope for his survival was gone, while his father assumed that Robert's mother and sister might be more inclined to keep him alive. His father had made the point again and again: "I never want to be on a ventilator. That's not life, Robert. It's better to just die than to be breathing through a tube."

But weeks before his death, he fell in the shower and the five-hour surgery on his leg was much longer than it should have been—the broken bone was between his father's previous knee and hip replacements, and both of those were a factor. And after so many hours of anesthesia, his father didn't regain consciousness. The doctors put him on a ventilator after the operation. It was standard procedure.

That night, Robert huddled with his wife, mother and sister in a hospital lounge that, like so many hospitals in Manhattan, had views of the East River and the skyline of Long Island City. They stared out the window and Robert said, "Let's decide this together. He didn't want to be on the ventilator. He would hate this. I think we should tell them to remove it tomorrow."

His mother and sister agreed. They'd heard Robert's father warn against being on a ventilator so many times, and Robert was glad to have unanimity on the issue.

But then there was a complication: Robert's father became conscious the next morning. He didn't know who he was or where he was, but this gave them all pause, as if there were still hope, and as if turning off the ventilator would be murder.

The next afternoon, Robert stood over his father and said, very slowly, as if talking to a child. "I'm going to tell you a story, Dad," and his father looked at him blankly. "You're here because you broke your leg getting out of the shower. And then you had to have an operation. It lasted five hours. Very long. And you were on anesthesia for five hours." Robert paused and watched his father's dawning insight into where he was and, perhaps, who Robert was.

And then Robert watched his father realize that he was hooked up to a ventilator and become visibly angry. It was as if his father suddenly found himself in a horror film, with a machine breathing for him and keeping him alive. He, a man who had always been fiercely independent, and who had always warned against such an outcome, now had the same sovereignty over his destiny as that of a potted plant, his life being extended through no choice of his own. Robert made eye contact with his mother and sister, and the family implicitly decided, for the second time, they had to do something.

They informed the staff.

His mother didn't want to be present for the end of her sixty-one-year marriage. She spent some intimate time with him, alone in the room. Then she went to the lounge.

Robert, his wife, and his sister were to be with his father to the end. They went into his room and the nurses told Robert and his sister that they had a final choice. They could ease up the morphine, which might allow Robert's father to become conscious and speak, but with the concurrent risk of his feeling pain. Or, they could increase the morphine and allow him to die in a soporific fog. Robert and his sister decided to decrease the morphine and the nurses followed their instructions.

After ten minutes, their father gradually regained consciousness and a nurse removed the breathing tube. He opened his eyes fully and he said only one thing: "Can you believe all of this?" meaning the tubes, the monitors, the machines and the fuss. Then he cried out, visibly in pain, Robert's sister gasped, and Robert signaled the nurses to increase the morphine, which they did—and his father died.

He and his sister spoke many times in the following months and their conversations were always the same.

"The nurses shouldn't have let him suffer," his sister would say.

"But it was our decision to ease him off the morphine, not the nurses', and he wasn't in pain for very long," Robert would reply.

"But he shouldn't have been in any pain at all," his sister would say, to which Robert finally said, "Suzanne, if you fall and scrape your knee you experience pain. He didn't fall and scrape his knee. He was actually dying, so wouldn't that involve a little pain? And it was just for a minute or two."

His sister didn't agree but Robert concluded that, on balance, he'd done right by his father.

By now all of the yoga practitioners lay on their mats for the last part of the class and they all turned to the right. Robert gazed at Donna on the next mat, the back of her head, her blond ponytail and her wet back. He wondered briefly about her life. He only knew his Wednesday yoga friends for one hour a week—though Donna, a designer, had once come to his new office after class and offered tips for how to arrange it—but then he felt dizzy, he'd run out of water. His mind went back to his sister, Suzanne, and the prospect of complaining about his father's nurses.

And then Robert felt something new regarding his father: the luxury of honoring his sister, as far as assigning blame in his father's final moments. Not that he'd objected to the nurses, they were innocent, nor to say that they caused his father to be in pain at the end, they didn't, but he mentally allowed for the first time that he, his father's proxy, had made a mistake that day.

He phrased it this way: *I did the wrong thing.*

And lying on his yoga mat, he suddenly felt guilt—an emotion Robert didn't often feel. Dad trusted me, he thought. He looked to me to make sure the end of his life was the way he wanted it to be, and I let him down. I can never change that.

What dread Robert felt just then. Yet he sensed there was something else going on: It was as if guilt had a vitality to it. He felt despair on his yoga mat, yes, but also strangely alive.

What was that about?

He ignored it and summed up his thoughts this way: my father designated me as his health-care proxy and specifically asked not to be on a ventilator, but he was.

Robert rolled onto his stomach and tried to mentally change the subject. He thought, I'll remember a pleasant memory between my father and me. He knew the events from the eulogy didn't count; he'd repeated them too many times in his head to serve his current purpose. They were too dry now. He needed something fresh.

What did my father and I have between us? Let's see, he thought, as he arched his back, pulled on his ankles and breathed through his nose. OK, here's one: he sent me to summer camp. But Robert soon realized that summer camp didn't involve actual memories with his father; he went to the Berkshires for two months each summer and his father was hundreds of miles away, at home, so he knew this was an empty memory of the two of them, just an idea, intellectual 1's and o's.

Then Robert pulled up memories of going to Giants games with his father in the freezing cold—how did they bear it? Robert drank soup from a thermos, his father drank whiskey from a flask, and they'd huddle together. How wonderful that was, but he asked himself, can I feel it? the closeness we had at the stadium? And the answer was no; the memories of those cold games were abstract, especially in the heat of the hot yoga class. It was all too long ago.

As he put his palms face-down under his abdomen and lifted his legs, he found his mind going to a strange place: he tried to remember a bad memory from his life with his father. Why? To feel a connection. Any connection at all.

There had been, what? career issues. His father hadn't wanted him to be a therapist and had tormented him about it for years. What had he said? Business is the only reality— and his father's words had resulted in Robert resisting his true path for a long time and, yes, that was his father's fault. But Robert finally did pursue psychotherapy and he dove into it with more passion than he probably would have done otherwise. So, he thought, Dad's antagonism actually spurred me on.

Robert rolled onto his back, pulled his knees to his chest, and remembered the time in his twenties when he was in love with a girl, Carolyn, and it hadn't worked out. His father had said something awful. What was it he'd said? Ah yes. He'd said, "I don't know why she'd want to be with you." How terrible of him. But now Robert justified it in his mind: I needed to grow past that relationship, and eventually we broke up and I did grow past it. As for Dad? He always underestimated me. But the thing is, he just didn't really know who I was; in fact, Dad didn't know where he ended and I began. And with Robert's newly mature understanding, the bad memory—his father's cruel remark about him—no longer stung.

Robert wrinkled his brow and thought, Even my bad memories of him are erased. Everything's erased, as the towers were.

He skimmed through his past to find another memory and then he came up with one: while he was standing over his father in those final days, telling him the story of how he'd ended up in the hospital, they'd held hands for the first time since Robert was a boy. That was a good one, yes—but, Robert thought, I can't feel it.

It was no use, he thought. The old man is so far gone.

The yoga class ended. He and his friend Lorenza made eye contact as she walked by him to exit the studio. She was an

Italian married to an American and they often talked before class—she had a cosmetics line—but after class no one talked; everyone was too drained.

Robert lay very still on his mat and, as he stared at the studio ceiling, he mentally repeated the things that were now so apparent:

My father didn't want to be on a ventilator, and he was, because of me.

He didn't need to suffer at the end, and he did, because of me.

And then things changed ... Robert found that by letting those thoughts wash over his tired, wet body, he suddenly felt more vital and alive.

He paused to once again register the strangeness of the experience.

What was it?

Then it was clear to him: By the force of this new emotion, one he rarely felt, his guilt, Robert momentarily succeeded at holding onto a man he'd almost forgotten.

IV

"I was thinking of how buildings become symbols," Paul said in his next session. "I don't mean to be gruesome, but structures take on lasting meanings. Buildings do. Even bridges. I mean, people kill themselves by jumping off them. The Empire State. The Golden Gate. Think of their families having to look at those structures afterward."

"It's terrible," Robert said.

"Right. It makes it hard for them to forget," Paul said. "And then the question is: Is it still the same building? The same bridge? Or has it become a symbol to the survivors? Do you see?"

Robert thought a moment and said, "I think I see. You're saying the Golden Gate Bridge becomes 'you were terrible to her,' every time the family looks at it. And even if they weren't terrible to her, that's what it suggests. Or the Empire State Building becomes 'you could have known, you could have stopped him,' every time they see it."

"Right," Paul said. "Imagine if I could design those things in. How would you design 'you were terrible to her!' into a building?"

"Well, I guess the question for us is: What does the Empire State become to you now? Or what did the World Trade Towers mean?" Robert said.

"The towers? The memory of those makes my head spin. They just disappeared," Paul said. "But the Empire State? That's easier. Richard and I kissed up there on our first date. So I look at the Empire State and it's about him, but now it also symbolizes: I was never all in."

"What do you mean?" Robert said.

Paul took a long moment and spoke deliberately.

"Richard's very ill. Dying. And he's not at home. He's at his brother's. His sister-in-law is a nurse. That's the separation I spoke of earlier," Paul said.

Robert sensed something false in Paul's tone of voice but he thought, Perhaps it's because he's finally telling me what's really happening, after all this time.

"Richard always said we were ridiculous with the age difference, remember?" Paul said. "He said it would be humiliating to have someone watch him get older, and when he became sick with cancer, and it got really bad, he went to stay with them."

"What's that like for you?" Robert said.

"I don't want to do that, Robert, the how does it make you feel? I want to go through my thoughts on the relationship. I can't talk about the rest yet."

"All right," Robert said.

"So, let's start with this: When Richard used to express his reservations about the age difference, I shushed him away. I told him age didn't matter. But I was too busy with a seduction, you see?"

"No," Robert said.

"I wanted him. Was I attracted to him? Yes. But Richard was a notch in my belt, too, especially because he was resisting. So it was a seduction, Robert, a win that I wanted and achieved. And also, he was a big deal in the industry, don't forget. So I knew being with him would benefit me on some level.

"I remember we went to Anguilla early on," Paul continued. "Stayed at Malliouhana, this great hotel. The deck where you eat breakfast, it's gorgeous, right on the water, that aqua water, and we'd sit there, reading the *Times* and eating our eggs and croissants. We also went deep-sea fishing on that trip. And I thought, This is perfect. He's going to be mine, this serious architect. But there was always the age difference. Richard's anxiety about that got under my skin— he wasn't the only one worried about it—but I didn't tell him. So I kept one foot in, one foot out."

"How so?" Robert said.

"In the early years I had a lover, Noah, whom I'd see on occasion. He was my age. I'd be with him and think, if Richard dies before me, I'll have Noah to go to. It lasted about five years, but imagine that I was thinking that way twenty years ago ...

"Also, there was this: I always wanted to know that if he died, I'd be OK, so I'd perpetually shop for apartments. I never told him. I had a real estate agent and I'd price out different places. I actually went to look at some.

"In the early years, I'd see what I could rent," he continued. "Then, later, as I became more successful, what I could buy. Because we weren't married, you see, we couldn't be married back then, so I had to think of us as impermanent, didn't I? One time, Richard saw the email from the agent and said, 'What's this?' I said, 'I like to keep my eye on the market.' He said, 'Don't you like it here, in this apartment?' at his place, at One Fifth. I said, 'I do.' So, Robert, as far as the Empire State Building, when I look at it now? I remember that we kissed there for the first time. But I also remember this: I used him."

"Did you really?" Robert said.

"Yes."

"For what?" Robert said.

"To get ahead."

"Did you love him?"

"Yes. Deeply."

"So, then?" Robert said.

"What are you saying?"

"Everyone uses everyone, Paul," Robert said. "It depends how you think of it."

"I need to tell you the rest," Paul said and Robert nodded.

"… Richard became ill," he continued. "I always thought he'd die of old age, Robert. I was ready for that. But this? After twenty years and he was only in his late sixties? He went to stay with his brother, as I said. He said he wanted to give me a break. And he's stayed for a while. You see? He didn't trust me to take care of him."

"Or he wanted to give you a break," Robert said.

"Perhaps. But what does it all mean?" Paul said. "I think that's why the World Trade Towers came to haunt me, Robert. They were about things disappearing, just the way I was in the relationship with Richard. I thought I could just find a new lover, as Noah had been, or even a new apartment. Maybe that I could be like you, Robert: your friendship with Graham ended, and I'd just come to realize that we'd had a good thing, and it had just expired. But I can't do that."

Robert looked at him. "Is Richard still at his brother's?"

"When your father died," Paul said, ignoring him, "you felt horrible, but you said he was old, so you didn't feel that bad."

Robert was silent.

"Do you ever feel bad? Or guilty?" Paul said.

Robert didn't answer.

"Oh, I'm sorry," Paul said.

"No, it's all right," Robert said, and his thoughts from the yoga class came back to him again, like a recording.

"Should we talk about something else?" Paul said.

Robert smiled and pulled his attention back into the room. "No, Paul. I'll answer. Do I feel bad? My father said he didn't want to be on a ventilator and he was, and I was his health-care proxy."

"But you said it was your father's time to go," Paul said. "He was old, right? Richard wasn't. So can you imagine how I feel?"

"How?"

Now Paul was silent and he shook his head and shrugged.

"Thank you, Paul," Robert said, after a moment.

"For what?"

"For what? For what you just led me to realize," Robert said. "The thing is, Paul: we make stuff up and it's true but it's also not."

"What?" Paul said.

"The question is if I did the best I could with my father, and I did ... I mean, it's complicated but, Paul, I did the best I could," Robert said, and he laughed. "Well, this seems like my therapy, Paul, not yours."

"Can you explain?"

"You loved Richard. And I think you've done the best you can."

"And my having a lover?"

"People have lovers."

"And my looking for apartments?"

"You didn't feel secure."

"Why?" Paul said.

"I don't know, Paul. Maybe from your past; from abandonment issues that we can explore," Robert said. "Or maybe because legally, as men, you couldn't be married, so you couldn't automatically inherit property. The point is, people feel insecure and they worry about abandonment, but they still have relationships, they still try, and you did."

Paul looked at him for a moment and said, "Remember how the 9/11 anniversary started all of this for me? When I remembered how those buildings just disappeared? On the anniversary of 9/11, it struck me then and there that if Richard could leave me, if he could just choose to be at his brother's, then I'd just have to wait. Suspended animation. I was numb."

"What else?"

"That's enough," Paul said.

The session was about to end.

"This may be an unusual request, Paul, but I wonder if I can see a picture of Richard, or of you and Richard?" Robert said.

"Look on my Instagram and you'll see it all."

"All right. I'll do it tonight," Robert said.

"Try not to fall in love with him, though."

That night, at home, Robert pulled up Paul's Instagram page. Most of the pictures were of the two of them. Richard seemed kind and Robert could see that Richard was clearly the elder. The two of them looked happy together, on a beach in Mexico, at a black-tie, and in ski sweaters at Christmas.

Robert was about to put his phone down, but then he decided to read the comments under a shot of them at what seemed like City Hall; they were in suits.

He read a few and suddenly looked away, stunned. Then he looked back.

Many of the comments were wishing Paul condolences.

Richard was dead. He died just months before.

I should have known that, Robert thought, but Paul had obviously been far from wanting to go there himself—until the 9/11 anniversary had made him think about things that disappeared.

Robert looked back at the phone and read another comment. It said: "So sorry about your husband."

He put down his phone.

They'd been married.

Robert got up to take a walk. His wife saw him by the door and, reading his face, said, "Is anything wrong?

He said, "No," and he went out, and walked through the Village for an hour.

◻ ◻ ◻

"I looked at your Instagram page," Robert said at the start of the next session.

Their eyes met, and Paul's filled with tears. "You looked at the page. And?"

Robert didn't reply.

"I see," Paul quietly said. "I'm sorry, Robert."

"You don't need to be. I understand."

Paul cried, and then he said, "I'll tell you the whole story."

"All right."

Paul paused for a moment and then he slowly began. "Richard became ill, I told you. He was falling apart. Dying. He went to stay with his brother. He said he wanted to give me a break. I felt he trusted them more than he did me. Or maybe he just didn't want me to see him that sick."

Robert nodded.

"And then he died," Paul said. "At his brother's. Unexpectedly. He'd only been there for eight days." His eyes narrowed. "They called me to go, and I saw him at the end, but he was already unconscious."

"I'm so sorry, Paul."

"And that's when I became invisible."

Robert sat very still. This was the first time that Richard was truly dead for both of them, together. Robert felt tears coming to his eyes as well. It was a moment of silence.

Finally, Paul spoke. "You said that people don't have to let someone go when they grieve, right? They can keep them in mind?"

"Yes," Robert said.

"So, here's the thing. Richard's not going to be gone until I decide that he is," Paul said.

Robert said quietly, "All right, Paul."

"I was half in, half out, and I can't just have him disappear," Paul said. "I need to reconstruct him before I can possibly let him go. To talk about him. So where do we start?"

They looked at each other and Paul was waiting.

Robert took out his phone and turned to Paul's Instagram page.

"I looked at these pictures last night. You two looked great together," Robert said.

Paul nodded.

"How about this one?" Robert said, and he pulled up a picture of them on a wooden deck, in front of an aqua sea. "Didn't you tell me about this trip?" He handed Paul the phone.

"Yes, that was in Anguilla. We'd eat breakfast there. Someone took the picture."

"Beautiful. Can you tell me more?" Robert said.

"Yes, I can."

Paul looked down at Robert's phone and lost himself in thought, crying and then smiling. He finally looked up and said, "Where should I start?"

Robert said, "Anywhere."

AFTERWORD

I am a psychotherapist in New York City.

This work has given me a sense of what makes people tick, and having a practice in New York has been breathtaking. My real-life patients have included mothers, fathers, film directors, TV actors, musicians, dancers, investment bankers, consultants, NFL players, NBA wives, doctors, lawyers, bakers covered in flour, robot designers, people having difficulties in relationships, people needing to break up, people divorcing, people meeting someone new, and people falling in love. I've also felt as if I were working at the United Nations, with patients who were Australian, Nigerian, English, French, Swedish, Danish, Spanish, Italian, Venezuelan, Brazilian, Chilean, Argentinian, Polish, Indian, Iraqi, Iranian and of course, American.

People have never ceased to amaze me.

□ □ □

I've always found being a psychotherapist a privilege—to enter into a therapeutic alliance with so many people, to have them share their inner worlds, to get to know them, and, ultimately, to be of assistance. From the beginning, I always wished people could know what it was like to sit in the chair and see the world through a therapist's eyes; the hard parts, yes, but also the wonder and magic of people's evolution.

This desire eventually led me to write these seven fictional stories.

"Robert," the therapist, is a character in these stories. This leads to a few essential questions. For one, is he good at his job? Well, I'm a bit biased, but I'd say he's excellent. But then there's this: he's also human, which presented a conundrum to me as a writer. In these stories Robert is, at times, filled with the kinds of thoughts and, yes, occasional anxieties or feelings of loss, that he has in common with every psycho-therapist on the planet, sooner or later, especially early in their careers—let's say, every therapist from New York to Sydney—but these are behind-the-curtain thoughts, hidden from public view.

I know the game: as psychotherapists, we're expected to present ourselves as less than fully human; often, as role models. But as I see it, I can do my job competently and fictional Robert can, while, in these stories, I can fantasize, imagine or attest to what Robert might be feeling in reaction to his patients.

To me, it's clear: along with the fascinating aspects of the work, there is the crucible, for every practitioner, of going deep into the sometimes bizarre world of the human mind, including that of his or her own.

So these stories, being as much about "Robert" as they are about his patients, may resonate the most for those who are therapists or patients in real life, but they are also intended as reflections on the inner life and how the wheels turn.

Finally, it's worth noting, again, that the patients in these stories are fictional. Jack, Kara, Jen, David, Jeremy, Catherine, James, and Paul are not anonymized versions of my patients nor of the situations of my patients' lives—but were wholly invented for this book. I created the stories and the characters for the fun of exploring a psychological riddle; or, in other cases, to give a portrait of what people go through; or, finally, to give a sense of what therapists experience in our daily rounds.

I've been told that fictional stories by a psychotherapist are not a genre, so I suppose the genre begins here.

ACKNOWLEDGMENTS

I'd like to thank Bob for everything, Bette and Joan for their love and support—and Bette for reading and giving feedback on these stories more times than any human should reasonably have to, Brother Satyananda and Beth Vesel for their early encouragement of the project, Lisa Halliday for the wisdom to lead me to Andy ... Andy Kifer and George Hammond for the brutal candor of their feedback, which was worth more, at the time, than a hundred pats on the back would have been, artist Terry Rosenberg for his cover drawing, Claudia Alvarez for her input, and, finally, master photographers John Taylor and Dianne Dubler, for forcing me to climb up and down a mountain with them during a pandemic for a cover photo.